Leadership and
Emotional Sabotage

LEADERSHIP

AND

EMOTIONAL SABOTAGE

RESISTING THE ANXIETY THAT WILL WRECK YOUR FAMILY, DESTROY YOUR CHURCH, AND RUIN THE WORLD

JOE RIGNEY

CANON PRESS

MOSCOW, IDAHO

Published by Canon Press
P.O. Box 8729, Moscow, Idaho 83843
800.488.2034 | www.canonpress.com

Joe Rigney, *Leadership and Emotional Sabotage: Resisting the Anxiety That Will Wreck Your Family, Destroy Your Church, and Ruin the World.* Copyright ©2024 by Joe Rigney.

Cover design by James Engerbretson.
Interior design by Valerie Anne Bost.

Some of the material in this book appeared in a previous form on desiringgod.org.

Printed in the United States of America.

Library of Congress Cataloging-in-Publication Data is on file with the publisher.

24 25 26 27 28 29 30 31 32 33   10 9 8 7 6 5 4 3 2 1

To Jonathan Parnell

CONTENTS

ACKNOWLEDGMENTS

THIS LITTLE BOOK WAS A DECADE IN THE making, and the lessons in it came through many hands. It's fitting that I express my gratitude to God for those hands here in the acknowledgements.

For my students at Bethlehem College and Seminary who joined me in plundering the Egyptians in order to build the house of God as we debated and discussed Edwin Friedman, Shakespeare, and the Bible. One of those students, Jake McAtee, now works for Canon Press and is responsible for bringing to light both this book and its companion course on Canon+.

For my former colleagues at Bethlehem College and Seminary who helped me to refine a vision for mature, sober-minded leadership, rooted in gravity and gladness in

Jesus Christ. In that regard, I'm especially grateful for Andy Naselli, Jason Abell, Jonathon Woodyard, Rick Segal, Brian Tabb, Zack Howard, and Clint Manley.

For Doug Wilson and Ben Merkle, with whom I have had many conversations about Friedman, leadership, and courage over the years.

For Ethan Oldham, whose editorial eye improved this book substantially.

For my wife Jenny and my three sons—Sam, Peter, and Jack—who have inspired and encouraged me in my efforts to become a steady, sober-minded leader in our home.

For the pastors at Cities Church, with whom I gladly served for nine years. Shepherding God's flock with them was a proving ground as we sought to lead our congregation with clarity, steadfastness, and vision.

In particular, I want to express my gratitude to God for my friend Jonathan Parnell. He is the sort of friend who faithfully presses home the reality that Jesus is real amidst all of the chaos, confusion, and hardships of life and ministry. He has been a constant reminder that Christ anchors us so that we become imperturbable—calm, collected, and steady no matter our circumstances. It's to him that I dedicate this book.

INTRODUCTION

WE LIVE IN AN AGE OF ANXIETY, CONFUSION, and turmoil. There's something "in the air" that feels highly combustible, a highly reactive atmosphere that pervades all institutions of society: from families to churches to businesses to governments. There's a sense that we're sitting on a powder keg—one small match and *kaboom*.

In other words, we live in an age of angst and agitation, marked by fierce anxiety storms that shoot through society, and reactive social stampedes that trample everything in their path. Our world demands that whole communities adapt to their most reactive, unstable, and immature members. We've turned blame-shifting and excuse-making into an art, so that hardly anyone takes responsibility for themselves, their emotions, their actions, and their situation.

Instead, we point fingers and throw stones at "those people" (whoever they are) because *they* are the real problem. We live in a culture constantly looking for a quick fix, a silver bullet, a magic spell that will solve all our problems.

As a result, the individuals and institutions that ought to act as shock absorbers in crisis are instead held hostage and paralyzed by indecision and failures of nerve. Leaders are bombarded by interest groups and agitators, and then put in impossible situations: "We need you to fix the problem, but you can't bring up the elephant in the room." As a result, they adopt appeasement strategies in order to avoid conflict. When entire institutions fall prey to this spirit of appeasement, paralysis, and excuse-making, the most mature and motivated members begin to quietly drift away, which just makes everything worse.

So what should we do about it?

For years, I've recommended Edwin Friedman's *A Failure of Nerve: Leadership in the Age of the Quick Fix* as an essential book for Christian leaders. The book is filled with clear-eyed observations about our societal sickness and the ways it manifests in our families, our churches, and our civic institutions. Friedman diagnoses our societal problem in terms of "chronic anxiety."

> Chronic anxiety is systemic; it is deeper and more embracing than community nervousness. Rather than something that resides within the psyche of each one, it is something that can envelop, if not actually connect, people. It is a regressive emotional process that is quite different from

the more familiar, acute anxiety we experience ovei
cific concerns. Its expression is not dependent on \
or events, even though specific happenings could seem
trigger it, and it has a way of reinforcing its own momen-
tum. Chronic anxiety might be compared to the volatile
atmosphere of a room filled with gas fumes. Any sparking
incident could set off a conflagration, yet rather than trying to disperse the fumes people blame the person who
struck the match.[1]

Friedman's solution to this society-wide sickness is what
he calls "well-differentiated leadership."

[A well-differentiated leader is] someone who has clarity
about his or her own life goals and, therefore, someone who
is less likely to become lost in the anxious emotional processes swirling about. I mean someone who can be separate
while still remaining connected and, therefore, can maintain
a modifying, non-anxious, and sometimes challenging presence. I mean someone who can manage his or her own reactivity in response to the automatic reactivity of others and,
therefore, be able to take stands at the risk of displeasing.[2]

"Differentiated" is a crucial term for Friedman. It sum-
marizes a number of qualities and characteristics that are
essential for healthy and effective leaders.

1. Edwin H. Friedman, *A Failure of Nerve: Leadership in the Age of the Quick Fix*, rev.
ed. (New York: Church Publishing, 2017), 65.
2. Friedman, *Failure of Nerve*, 15.

- Differentiation refers to a direction in life rather than a state of being.
- Differentiation is the capacity to take a stand in an intense emotional system.
- Differentiation is saying "I" when others are demanding "we."
- Differentiation is containing one's reactivity to the reactivity of others, which includes the ability to avoid being polarized.
- Differentiation is maintaining a non-anxious presence in the face of anxious others.
- Differentiation is knowing where one ends and another begins.
- Differentiation is being able to cease automatically being one of the system's emotional dominoes.
- Differentiation is being clear about one's own personal values and goals.
- Differentiation is taking maximum responsibility for one's own emotional being and destiny rather than blaming others or the context.[3]

All of this is helpful. Friedman was a Jewish rabbi, and in some respects, his mind ran in biblical ruts. As a result, many of his insights track with biblical principles.

However, as much as I appreciate Friedman, his theology and anthropology are lacking in some significant ways. He advocates a form of process theology, and his commitment to evolutionary biology is apparent throughout the book. As

3. Friedman, *Failure of Nerve*, 195.

a result, readers have to wade through piles of dodgy theology and evolutionary gobbledygook in order to get the good stuff. What's more, Friedman tends to operate with a specialized clinical vocabulary that often requires translation into more biblical language. What Friedman calls "self-differentiation with a non-anxious presence," the Bible calls "sober-mindedness." What Friedman calls "reactivity," the Bible calls "passions." "People-pleasing" and "fear of man" are the biblical terms for what Friedman calls "herding." And so on.

This book is my attempt to do justice to Friedman's insights while grounding them in the Scriptures, and extending and applying them in the home, the church, and the world.

The structure is simple. In Chapter 1, I use Shakespeare, Friedman, and the book of Genesis to diagnose our cultural sickness. In Chapter 2, I propo-se a biblical cure, oriented by the fifth, the tenth, and the first commandments. In Chapter 3, I summarize key challenges to biblical leadership. Chapters 4–6 then show what faithful, sober-minded leadership looks like in the home, the church, and the world.

My hope and prayer is that God will use this simple book to encourage and strengthen Christian leaders to fulfill their calling by leading with gravity and gladness, with sober-mindedness and maturity, with steady purpose and deep joy, so that we rebuild the walls of Christendom and show forth the excellencies of the living God in the joy and gladness of our families, our churches, our schools, and our communities.

CHAPTER 1

A SHAKESPEAREAN POWDER KEG

AS WE TRY TO MAKE SENSE OF OUR CULTURAL moment, we often find ourselves baffled. Families, churches, and communities have been inexplicably torn apart by divisions and conflict. People who once were like-minded and engaged in shared projects find themselves incapable of working together. Many of us have watched in dismay as people we know—family members, church members, neighbors— have drifted, or even jumped headlong into foolishness and sin. We've seen otherwise godly pastors coddling sin and error and catering to agitators. Institutional leaders walk on eggshells in their board rooms because of the crackle in the air. Government officials jump from crisis to crisis, and seem constitutionally incapable of making wise decisions. There's a palpable sense that no one is in charge, and no one knows what to do.

Everyone wants to blame the internet. Social media, they say, is responsible for the fracturing of our communities and the polarized tribalism that surrounds us. And there are material, economic, social, and technological factors that have contributed to this age of agitation: the Industrial Revolution, followed by the Sexual Revolution and Digital Revolution; the expansion of mobility, globalization, migration, and so on. And our technologies undoubtedly contribute to what ails us. They amplify and reinforce our spiritual and social sickness.

But the problem runs deeper than Twitter, Facebook, and cable news.

And so as we think about living in the midst of the Great Unraveling, in an age of anxiety, agitation, and turmoil, I want to begin our diagnosis in perhaps a surprising place. I want to begin with Shakespeare.

THE FOUNDATION OF SOCIAL ORDER

One of Shakespeare's lesser-known plays is *Troilus and Cressida*. It retells the story of the Trojan War, featuring many of the heroes from Homer's epic poem.

In Act 1, Scene 3, the Greek generals are discussing why it is taking so long for them to defeat Troy. Despite seven years of war, they are no closer to victory. Agamemnon, the supreme leader of the Greek forces, attributes their difficulty to the "trials of great Jove,"[1] who seeks to prove their constancy and mettle with adversity and hardship. Apart from such tests, there is no distinction between the bold and the coward, the wise and the fool, the hard and the soft. Trials separate the true men from the pretenders. Nestor, an older general, echoes his analysis: "In the reproof of chance [i.e. fortune] lies the true proof of men."[2] When the seas are smooth and the waves placid, even girly men will sail. But when the North Wind howls and the tempests rage, you see who the true sailors are. "Valour's *show* and valour's *worth* divide in storms of fortune."[3] According to both generals, the reason that the Greek army has been unable to conquer Troy is because the gods are testing them with trials and hardships. For these generals, the reasons for their failure are external.

And perhaps Agamemnon and Nestor have a point. External challenges do matter. But then Ulysses speaks and offers a very different analysis, concluding that Troy still stands, not because of its own strength, but because of a particular sickness among the Greeks. The problem, he says, is not external, but internal. And most importantly for our purposes, the sickness that Ulysses describes infects not only armies, but entire societies—including our own.

1. William Shakespeare, *Troilus and Cressida*, ed. Kenneth Muir (New York: Oxford University Press, 1982), 1.3.19.
2. Shakespeare, *Troilus and Cressida*, 1.3.32–33.
3. Shakespeare, *Troilus and Cressida*, 1.3.45–46.

Troy, yet upon his bases, had been down,

And the great Hector's sword had lacked a master,

But for these instances:

The specialty of rule hath been neglected,

And look how many Grecian tents do stand

Hollow upon this plain, so many hollow factions.

When that the general is not like the hive,

To whom the foragers shall all repair,

What honey is expected? Degree being vizarded,

Th'unworthiest shows as fairly in the mask.

The heavens themselves, the planets, and this centre

Observe degree, priority, and place,

Insisture, course, proportion, season, form,

Office, and custom, in all line of order.

And therefore is the glorious planet Sol

In noble eminence enthroned and sphered

Amidst the other; whose med'cinable eye

Corrects the influence of evil planets,

And posts like the commandment of a king,

Sans check to good and bad. But when the planets

In evil mixture to disorder wander,

What plagues, and what portents, what mutiny,

What raging of the sea, shaking of earth,

Commotion in the winds, frights, changes, horrors,

Divert and crack, rend and deracinate

The unity and married calm of states

Quite from their fixure! O, when degree is shaked,

Which is the ladder of all high designs,

The enterprise is sick! How could communities,

Degrees in schools, and brotherhoods in cities,

Peaceful commerce from dividable shores,

The primogeniture and due of birth,

Prerogative of age, crowns, sceptres, laurels,

But by degree stand in authentic place?

Take but degree away, untune that string,

And hark what discord follows. Each thing meets

In mere oppugnancy. The bounded waters

Should lift their bosoms higher than the shores,

And make a sop of all this solid globe;

Strength should be lord of imbecility,

And the rude son should strike his father dead.

Force should be right; or rather, right and wrong,

Between whose endless jar justice recides,

Should lose their names, and so should justice too.

Then everything includes itself in power,

Power into will, will into appetite;

And appetite, an universal wolf,

So doubly seconded with will and power,

Must make perforce an universal prey,

And last eat up himself. Great Agamemnon,

This chaos, when degree is suffocate,

Follows the choking.

And this neglection of degree it is

That by a pace goes backward with a purpose

It hath to climb. The general's disdained

By him one step below, he by the next,

That next by him beneath; so every step,

Exampled by the first pace that is sick

Of his superior, grows to an envious fever
Of pale and bloodless emulation.
And 'tis this fever that keeps Troy on foot,
Not her own sinews. To end a tale of length,
Troy in our weakness stands, not in her strength.[4]

The key concept in Ulysses's speech is what he calls "Degree." Degree is the principle of cultural order or rule or hierarchy. It includes things like "priority, and place, insisture, course, proportion, season, form, office, and custom, in all line of order." It's the organizing principle of a social body, and is therefore essential to all social purposes; in Ulysses's words, it is "the ladder of all high designs." Communities, schools, guilds and businesses, trade between nations, peaceful relationships between generations, political order, and social merit all stand in their true place "by degree."

We might put it this way. Every society has relationships of difference: husband-wife, parent-child, customer-merchant, employer-employee, teacher-student, magistrate-citizen, elders-youth, pastor-congregation. Within a given society, there is a kind of family resemblance in all of these different relationships. There is a quality, an atmosphere, a common thread, that integrates and ties all of these various relationships together. This is Degree (with a capital D). It's the bond or glue that keeps people separate but connected, distinct yet related. It's the cadence that regulates a culture's rhythms and seasons, its offices and customs, its sense of propriety and justice.

4. Shakespeare, Troilus and Cressida, 1.3.74–136.

Once you notice it, Ulysses's idea of Degree turns up everywhere—and of course, this is because God made the world in a particular way. We see Degree in God's ordering of creation in Genesis 1. God separates light from darkness, but then binds them together as Day and Night. He separates earth and heavens, seas and land, fish and birds and beasts, and each of these according to their kinds. There are many separations and differences and distinctions that God makes, but they're all a part of one majestic whole, one natural order, one Cosmos.

Degree in the natural world finds its counterpart in the social world. As C.S. Lewis said, "I do not believe that God created an egalitarian world. I believe the authority of parent over child, husband over wife, learned over simple to have been as much a part of the original plan as the authority of man over beast."[5]

Degree is often embodied in a particular authority or authorities. In a tribal society, this might be the chief or the shaman. In an army, it's the general. In a monarchy, it's the king. In our society, it might be the president or perhaps all three branches of our government as an institution. Within the family, it's the husband or father.

Ulysses uses a number of metaphors to describe Degree. He depicts it using the sun and the solar system. Degree operates like gravity, regulating the orbit of all of the planets so that they don't collide with one another, so that their heavenly dance is flawless and harmonious. Planets orbit the sun, and

5. C. S. Lewis, "Membership" in *The Weight of Glory: And Other Addresses* (New York: HarperOne, 2001), 168.

moons orbit the planets. In the same way, families, churches, businesses, and states orbit around fathers, ministers, bosses, and kings. Degree, then, operates in the invisible and mysterious way that gravity or magnetism does in the natural order.

Or, to use a different analogy, Degree is like the melody line in a symphony that guides and governs the harmony of the song. The different spheres of society are the different categories of instruments: strings, woodwinds, brass, and percussion. Each section has a representative leader—the first chair—who leads and guides the rest of the musicians in their performance.

CRISIS OF DEGREE

This is how Degree ought to function. But in a fallen world, it frequently doesn't. Why not? According to Ulysses, Degree can be neglected, vizarded (or concealed), shaked, untuned, and suffocated. With what result? When the specialty of rule (i.e., the bonds of authority) is neglected, all you're left with are hollow factions. When degree is shaked, enterprise (ambition) is sick. Untune the string of degree, and hark, what discord follows. When degree is suffocated, chaos follows the choking. To be more concrete, when Degree collapses, soldiers are ineffective in battle, as envy and rivalry spread through the ranks like fever, resulting in either internal conflict or aimless malaise. That's why the Greek armies have failed to conquer Troy.

When gravity weakens, the planets wander and mutiny and collide with one another. When the melody line of a song is lost, and the instruments are at odds with each other, then harmony turns into cacophony, beautiful music into noise and clamor. We see a return to chaos, like when a river overflows its banks, and moist air from above cools into fog. There's no difference between water and land and sky. All is one big soppy, cloudy mess.

When Degree is lost, "each thing meets in mere oppugnancy" (total antagonism), and everything breaks down: the strong prey on the weak, and the unthinkable becomes common (Ulysses mentions patricide as his example). Shakespeare echoes this thought in a similar passage in *King Lear*. What happens when the social order unravels? "Love cools, friendship falls off, brothers divide; in cities, mutinies, in countries, discords; in palaces, treason; and the bond crack'd 'twixt son and father."[6]

According to Ulysses, in the midst of a crisis of Degree, might makes right. Right and wrong lose their names; they become arbitrary. Justice becomes an empty term. Then everything is reduced to power. And power is reduced further into will or choice. And will is reduced into appetite (that is, to instinct and base desires). And appetite, amplified by power and will, becomes a wolf looking for prey, that in the end, devours itself.

What could cause such a destructive confusion, such self-devouring chaos? Ulysses attributes it to a kind of neglect or abdication. The "specialty of rule"—the bonds, obligations, and duties of authority—is neglected, and the whole body

---

6. William Shakespeare, *King Lear*, ed. Grace Ioppolo (New York: W.W. Norton, 2008), 1.2.100-102.

becomes sick with an envious fever. Abdication at the top leads to insubordination at the bottom. The general, Ulysses says, is disdained by the one below him, and the colonel by the one below him, and so on. This lack of honor spreads like an "envious fever of pale and bloodless emulation."

Degree enables generational progress and stability. It allows people to find their place, and (potentially) to move up. Fathers can hand off the family business to the son. Soldiers can rise from privates to sergeants to captains. The student becomes a professor. By binding different people together, Degree preserves order while allowing for change and transition.

But in the absence of Degree, envy and rivalry are cataclysmically released until total antagonism reduces us to appetite and self-devouring.

René Girard, a literary critic, compellingly argues that Shakespeare intends for us to see this self-devouring in terms of scapegoating. All of the pent-up conflicts, bitter rivalries, and discord that are unleashed in a Crisis of Degree eventually coalesce into a universal wolf that devours a sacrificial lamb, a scapegoat. In the end, there will be blood.

One of Shakespeare's most poignant scenes to this effect occurs in *Julius Caesar*. In the play, a group of senators, led by Cassius and Brutus, conspire together to assassinate Caesar, lest he become a tyrant (though it's evident that envy and rivalry are central motives as well). Following the murder, Mark Antony, Caesar's right-hand man, stirs up the Roman populace against the conspirators and a civil war breaks out. In the chaos that follows, Cinna the poet (who unhappily shares a first name with one of the conspiring senators) is found by a mob. This scene depicts the endgame of a crisis of Degree.

Cinna the Poet. I dreamt tonight that I did feast with Caesar,
>   And things unluckily charge my fantasy.
>   I have no will to wander forth of doors,
>   Yet something leads me forth.

1 Plebeian. What is your name?

2 Plebeian. Whither are you going?

3 Plebeian. Where do you dwell?

4 Plebeian. Are you a married man or a bachelor?

2 Plebeian. Answer every man directly.

1 Plebeian. Ay, and briefly.

4 Plebeian. Ay, and wisely.

3 Plebeian. Ay, and truly, you were best.

Cinna the Poet. What is my name? Whither am I going?
>   Where do I dwell? Am I a married man or a bach-
>   elor? Then to answer every man directly and briefly,
>   wisely and truly. Wisely I say I am a bachelor.

2 Plebeian. That's as much as to say they are fools that
>   marry. You'll bear me a bang for that, I fear.
>   Proceed directly.

Cinna the Poet. Directly I am going to Caesar's funeral.

1 Plebeian. As a friend or an enemy?

Cinna the Poet. As a friend.

2 Plebeian. That matter is answered directly.

4 Plebeian. For your dwelling—briefly.

Cinna the Poet. Briefly, I dwell by the Capitol.

> **3 Plebeian.** Your name, sir, truly.
>
> **Cinna the Poet.** Truly, my name is Cinna.
>
> **1 Plebeian.** Tear him to pieces, he's a conspirator.
>
> **Cinna the Poet.** I am Cinna the poet, I am Cinna the poet.
>
> **4 Plebeian.** Tear him for his bad verses, tear him for his bad verses.
>
> **Cinna the Poet.** I am not Cinna the conspirator.
>
> **4 Plebeian.** It is no matter, his name's Cinna. Pluck but his name out of his heart and turn him going.
>
> **3 Plebeian.** Tear him, tear him! Come, brands ho, fire-brands! To Brutus', to Cassius', burn all! Some to Decius' house, and some to Casca's, some to Ligarius'! Away, go![7]

Once unleashed, the envious fever will use any pretext to justify violence. The mob is a panic in search of a trigger, and in this case, the fact that a man shares a conspirator's name is sufficient.

So then, according to Ulysses, if we are in a Crisis of Degree, we should expect to see

1. a breakdown of authority across the various spheres of society;

2. a cascade of bitter rivalries and envy, mirror images of each other; and

3. multiplying accusations, blame-shifting, and scapegoating.

7. William Shakespeare, *Julius Caesar*, ed. Marvin Spevack (New York: Cambridge University Press, 1989), 3.3.1-34.

And all of this, Ulysses says, flows from the neglect of Degree, from the abdication of the leaders.

EDWIN FRIEDMAN ON AN ANXIOUS SOCIETY

Ulysses's diagnosis of the Greeks' problem dovetails nicely with Friedman's account of our cultural breakdown. He describes five key characteristics of our chronically anxious and agitated society. These features mark not only society as a whole, but also afflict the various institutions of society—families, churches, businesses, and the state.

1. Reactivity: an unending cycle of intense reactions of each member to events and to one another. This reactivity takes many forms. Some people blow up; others shut down. But whether over-reactive and hysterical or passive-aggressive and checked-out, the common thread is that the passions of the members govern and dictate both the mood of the body and its direction. The atmosphere of the institution is volatile, as though there are gas fumes ready to ignite at the stroke of a match.

2. Herding: a process where togetherness triumphs over individuality and everyone adapts to the least mature members of the community. The cycle of reactivity leads institutions to live in a constant state of tension. The goal becomes "peace" at all costs, otherwise known as appeasement. "Don't rock the boat" is the slogan, and it is wielded against the community's

leaders, who are expected to take responsibility not only for their own actions, but for the (re)actions of others. Disruptions by the immature will be accommodated; anyone who seeks to take a stand will be characterized as cruel, heartless, insensitive, unfeeling, uncooperative, selfish, and cold. As a result, the most immature members of a community come to set the agenda for the whole.

3. Blame displacement: an emotional state in which members of the community focus on forces that have victimized them rather than taking responsibility for their own being and destiny. One crucial mark of maturity is taking responsibility for oneself. On the other hand, immaturity involves blame-shifting and excuse-making. Blame displacement often takes the form of scapegoating. Typically this means exaggerating the influence and impact of one person at the expense of another. One person's contribution to the situation is blown out of proportion; the other's is minimized and down-played. This often produces a kind of social cohesion, as members of the group unite against the scapegoat.

4. Quick-fix mentality: a desire for symptom relief rather than fundamental change, flowing from a low threshold for pain. Broken institutions frequently choose long-term chronic pain rather than short-term acute pain that would actually address the issue. They look for solutions in data and information, rather than in

clarity and intentional action. Frequently they jump from expert to expert in search of the magic "how-to."

5. Failure of nerve: a lack of mature, decisive leadership. This problem both stems from and contributes to the first four. Leaders are bombarded by interest groups and agitators, and thus are constantly taken off mission. An empathetic paralysis sets in as everybody seeks to appease the most reactive members. The most motivated members of a community grow discouraged and exhausted by never-ending drama. The body is shot through with conflict, rivalry, and confusion. Eventually the leaders check out or burn out, and the community drifts along, tossed about by the passions of its members.

Both Shakespeare and Friedman identify a failure of nerve as central to the unraveling of the social order. Degree is neglected, anxiety and agitation multiply, and the body grows sick with envious fever. But more importantly for us, this diagnosis accords with a repeated biblical pattern.

ADAM IN THE GARDEN

We see the first and foundational failure of nerve in Genesis 3. Adam was called by God to work and keep the Garden, to protect and guard the sacred space. But when a serpent approaches his wife and blasphemes his God, Adam is passive. He just stands there and watches it happen. We know he was there because the passage says that "She gave some to her husband *who was with her*" (3:6). He ought to have picked up a sword to kill the dragon and protect the girl. But he doesn't. He's passive. He abdicates. He neglects his God-given responsibilities.

And this initial abdication and neglect leads to much greater evil. After Eve seizes and eats the forbidden fruit, she offers some to her husband. Now Adam has a choice—and his choice is different than Eve's. Eve wasn't around when God gave the command about the tree. She learned it (presumably) from Adam. The serpent exploited that weakness in order to deceive her. But Adam cannot be deceived here. He heard the Law of the Garden from God's own mouth. His choice is between God and his wife, between bone of his bone, and the One who made his bones.

And he chooses her.

He exchanges the glory of the immortal God for a creature. That's what God says when he punishes Adam: "You have listened to the voice of your wife and eaten of the tree of which I commanded you, 'You shall not eat it.'" In other words, "You listened to her and not to me. You listened to a creature, and not your Creator. You loved her and wanted her more than you loved me." This is high-handed idolatry. This is where drifting, where neglect, where abdication always leads. Eventually, you're faced with the big decision, and when the moment of Choice comes, you seize sin with a high hand.

But the pattern isn't yet complete. Abdication leads to Idolatry, and Idolatry gives way to Blame-shifting. When

God confronts Adam in his disobedience, he immediately passes the buck. "The woman you gave me." It's Eve's fault, and God's. It's everybody's fault except Adam's.

Think about what Adam blaming his wife means here. What was the consequence for eating? Death. "In the day you eat of it, you shall surely die." So, when Adam blames Eve, he is effectively saying, "Kill her, not me." He is supposed to protect her; instead he exposes her to judgment. He's supposed to die for her. Instead, he tries to make her die for him.

And then of course, she follows his example. God turns to her and says, "What is this that you have done?" She says, "The serpent deceived me, and I ate." Eve imitates Adam in the blame game.

This is the pattern—Abdication, Idolatry, Blame-shifting. It shows up again and again in the Scriptures. Aaron and the golden calf in Exodus 32. Saul and the Amalekites in 1 Samuel 15. It's this abdication of leadership, this neglect of the duties and responsibilities of authority, this failure of nerve that lies at the root of our cultural crisis.

So how do we fix it?

CHAPTER 2

BE SOBER-MINDED OR ELSE

IN THE FIRST CHAPTER, WE NOTED THAT we live in an age of agitation and angst marked by raging anxiety storms and fierce social stampedes, a blame-shifting and scapegoating society always in search of a quick fix. With Shakespeare's help, we explored our social situation in terms of a crisis of Degree, a breakdown and unraveling of social order in which neglect and abdication lead to rivalry, conflict, and chaos. In the absence of gravity, planets wander to disorder. Untune the string of Degree, and hark what discord follows. And we connected this abdication and neglect to the biblical pattern in the garden: Adam was passive and abdicated; then he committed high treason and idolatry; and then he scapegoated his wife and blamed God for his failures.

Now, in Ulysses's speech, he likens the Crisis of Degree to sickness: "When Degree is shaked, enterprise is sick." The neglect and abdication of leadership and authority cascades down through the ranks like a fever of envy, rivalry, and conflict. In this chapter, we'll sketch the outlines of a threefold cure for this fever, organizing the prescription by three of the Ten Commandments: the Fifth, the Tenth, and the First.

HONOR YOUR FATHER AND MOTHER

Degree, at the human level, has to do with ordered relationships. In other words, it has to do with asymmetry and hierarchy. In biblical terms, such concerns fall under the Fifth Commandment: honor your father and mother. Theologians have long rooted all social duties and responsibilities in this basic familial duty. For example, the Westminster Larger Catechism identifies the "father and mother" of the commandment as "not only natural parents, but all superiors in age and gifts, and especially such as, by God's ordinance, are over us in place of authority, whether in family, church, or commonwealth" (WLC 124). This means that the general scope of the fifth commandment includes "those duties which we mutually owe in our several relations, as inferiors, superiors, or equals" (WLC 126).

In light of this, the first element of the cure involves recovering a vision for body life that includes both faithful headship and faithful membership. The Scriptures regularly use the metaphor of a body to speak about human social life. The church is the body of Christ, with many members (1 Cor. 12). Marriage is a "one flesh" union—that is, one whole body that is made up of a head and a body (Eph. 5:22–30). In fact, we can consider the whole household in bodily terms, with the husband as the head and the wife and children as the various distinct members. For the moment, we'll focus largely on the household, though these principles are relevant for any type of social body: church, school, business, or state.

Let's begin with the obvious. The head and body are profoundly interdependent. You can't have one without the other. No one wants a bodiless head or a headless body. As God himself said in Genesis 2:18, "It is not good that the man should be alone." Thus, from the outset, our goal is to recognize how deeply woven together headship and bodyship must be. Head and body are complementary; they fit each other.

Additionally, the whole body has a purpose, a mission. In Genesis 1, the mission of the initial household is to be fruitful, multiply, fill the earth and subdue it, and have dominion over its inhabitants. The body as a whole does not exist for its own sake, but for the sake of God's mission in the world.

With these two truths in mind, let's reflect on the function of the head in relation to the body. We can summarize the head's role under two headings, one largely internal and the other largely external.

First, the head (in this case, the husband) orders or structures the whole body for its purpose through his presence, words, and actions, and empowers the members of the body to fulfill their calling.

Second, the head maintains the body's boundaries, represents the body to other bodies, and is responsible for the well-being of the body as a whole.

The head organizes and orders the body for its purpose. He orients the body and directs the body. Therefore, the head must have mission clarity; he must know what the mission *is* and what it *isn't.* He must know the body's purpose, and keep that purpose in mind as he empowers the body with his presence.

I stress the notion of "presence," because the head orients and directs the body the way that the earth orients and directs the moon. There's the image again: like a planet with its moon, a husband guides his home through his gravity. If he does so faithfully, the moon orbits properly. If he is unfaithful, the moon wanders into disorder.

Or we might use the musical image. The head sets the melody, including the tone, the tune, and the rhythm. It may be a melody line that enables glorious harmony. Or it may be off-beat and out of tune and result in nothing but noise. But one way or the other, the head establishes the melody.

In a similar vein and in keeping with the metaphor of the body, Friedman describes leaders as the immune system for the body. An immune system doesn't merely fight off infection; it first regulates the body's functions and processes; it maintains the body's integrity and boundaries, and it's through this integrity that the immune system then defends the body from sickness by recognizing and marshaling resources to fend off an infection.

Turn then to the notion of bodyship (or membership). Like headship, the body's role can be summarized in terms of internal and external dimensions.

First, the body receives the initiating presence, words, and actions of the head and refines them by providing feedback, input, and counsel to the head.

Second, the body glorifies the head's efforts and makes them fruitful by keeping in step with the head, carrying out the head's will and extending and amplifying the whole body's influence in the world.

Consider first the body's influence on the head through feedback and counsel. This is an inescapable truth; the body will do this, for good or for ill. Adam listened to the voice of his wife, and they fell into grave evil. Nabal did *not* listen to the voice of his wife (Abigail), and he fell into grave evil (1 Sam. 25). A husband is the head, and he can lead his family into ruin (like Adam) or into glory (like Jesus). In a similar way, a wife is the body, and she can influence the head for misery (like Eve) or for good (like the woman in Proverbs 31).

The book of Proverbs helps us to see the crucial role of influence and counsel. The book itself is counsel from a father to a son, a king to a prince. The prince has two quests: seek wisdom, and seek an excellent wife. And so throughout the book, a double choice is before him. Listen to Lady Wisdom or to Lady Folly. Pursue the Excellent Wife or the Adulterous Woman.

The prince is a head-in-training; he will order and structure and guide and direct his kingdom. But he is not autonomous or self-sufficient; he will be influenced, one way or another. And so he must choose his influences wisely. Thus, after he hearkens to the voice of Lady Wisdom for thirty chapters, the Excellent Wife walks down the aisle in Proverbs 31.

But the body doesn't merely provide clarifying counsel and feedback to the head. The body also is the place of fruitfulness. This is a fundamental truth: the body receives in order to give more. It does not just receive and return. It receives and glorifies. It receives and beautifies. It receives and amplifies. The one-flesh union of marriage again gives us the perfect instance of this fruitfulness in procreation. The husband is the gardener, and his wife is the garden. He sows his seed; she receives it and bears "fruit" (that is, children).

This is the calling of the body—to take what is good and make it better. To modify the metaphor of the planets, the head is like the sun and the body is like the moon, reflecting and extending the sun's light where the sun is not. Or to use the musical metaphor, the head establishes the melody, but the body provides the harmony and makes the song glorious. The head empowers, but the body uses that power to enlarge the domain of the household.

Here then is a vision of social harmony, with faithful leaders guarding, guiding, directing, and ordering the body through their presence, and then faithful members responding, giving counsel and feedback, and making the body fruitful in the world.

YOU SHALL NOT COVET

Such is the harmonious vision of social order protected by the Fifth Commandment. But beneath the well-ordered society lies the well-ordered soul. Here we move from the fifth commandment to the tenth. "You shall not covet"—that is, you must not give your desires free rein. You must order and govern your loves and appetites. Your passions and emotions must not lead you astray. And this is especially the case for heads: husbands, fathers, pastors, leaders, rulers.

If we live amidst raging anxiety storms and reactive social stampedes, the fundamental virtue leaders need is sober-mindedness. The Bible regards sober-mindedness as a key element of Christian maturity and a fundamental qualification for leadership. It shows up prominently in 1 Timothy 3 in the list of qualifications for church office. Here are some relevant passages:

> Therefore an overseer must be above reproach, the husband of one wife, sober-minded, self-controlled, respectable, hospitable, able to teach. (1 Tim. 3:2)

> Their wives likewise must be dignified, not slanderers, but sober-minded, faithful in all things. (1 Tim. 3:11)

> As for you, always be sober-minded, endure suffering, do the work of an evangelist, fulfill your ministry. (2 Tim. 4:5)

Literally, the term is "sobriety," as in the opposite of drunkenness. And drunkenness is a good launching point for understanding this virtue. Drunkenness involves the impairment of our physical abilities (staggering, loss of balance, slurred speech, etc.) as well as the impairment of our mental abilities and moral judgment (lack of inhibition and self-control such that it is easier to commit other sins). When we're drunk on alcohol, we neither see clearly nor act wisely.

But here's the crucial truth: we can be drunk on more than alcohol. We suffer the same sort of mental and moral impairment when we are overwhelmed by our passions and the passions of others. Think of the way that anxiety or anger can cloud your vision. Your passions, emotions, and reactions rise and fall violently so that your judgment is impaired. Or think of the way that your spouse's unhappiness and disapproval affects your ability to make wise decisions. The passions and reactions of other people can be so intense that you can't see clearly and as a result you're tossed about.

What are passions? At the most basic level, they are our immediate and impulsive desires. Paul links them closely to our bodies: "Let not sin reign in your mortal body, to make you obey its passions" (Rom. 6:12). Peter does too: "I urge you to abstain from the passions of the flesh, which wage war against your soul" (1 Pet. 2:11). Later, Peter puts them side-by-side with things like sensuality, sexual immorality, drunkenness, and lawless idolatry (1 Pet. 4:3). They deceive us (Eph. 4:22), lead us astray (2 Tim. 3:6), and enslave us (Titus 3:3). They have a direction; they want to take us somewhere. If we follow them, then we are indulging or gratifying our passions. We are being conformed to our passions.

Typically, we think of passions as the almost knee-jerk responses to good and bad things. And that's true as far as it goes. When you see something good, you immediately want it. When you see something bad, you immediately reject it.

When you see something frightening, you immediately fear it. When you see something that keeps you from getting what you want, you immediately get angry. Passions include these immediate impulses and snap reactions like anger, fear, desire, pity, or sadness.

But it's important to note that passions take many forms. Yes, we're in the grip of them when we're emotional, when they are intense and manifest and obvious. But dogged passivity can also be a reactive passion. We're led by our passions both when we blow up and when we shut down, when we get aggressive, and when we get passive-aggressive.

More than that, passions aren't always intense. They don't always operate at a fever pitch. They can be driving the show when they're on a slow-burn. When our passions are on a slow-burn and when they're vague and general, we often call them moods or attitudes. When we experience low-grade, long-term anger, we say that we're *frustrated*. When we experience low-grade, long-term fear, we say that we're *anxious* or worried. When it's vague and unidentified sadness, we're *depressed*. Or we just roll it all together and say that we're *stressed*. Whenever we use the language of angst, frustration, anxiety, depression, or stress, we're talking about passions on a low-boil, but often ready to erupt at the slightest trigger.

These passions were meant to be guided and governed by our minds which were meant to be guided and governed by God: God over mind, mind over passions. But in our sinfulness, everything gets turned upside down. We conform ourselves to our passions. Wherever our passions want to go, our minds follow. We are enslaved to our passions, led astray by our passions, *drunk* on our passions.

Which brings us back to sober-mindedness. Sober-mindedness includes at least three elements: clarity of mind, stability of soul, and readiness to act.

(1) Clarity of mind. Our passions act like fog. Anger, fear, pity, and desire distort our vision so that we don't see clearly. But when we are sober-minded, our vision is not clouded. Or change the metaphor. Consider how sobriety is often paired with wakefulness. In 1 Thessalonians 5, Paul echoes Jesus about the day of the Lord coming like a thief in the night. Then he says:

> But you are not in darkness, brothers, for that day to sur-prise you like a thief. For you are all children of light, chil-dren of the day. We are not of the night or of the dark-ness. So then let us not sleep, as others do, but let us keep awake and be sober. For those who sleep, sleep at night, and those who get drunk, are drunk at night. But since we belong to the day, let us be sober, having put on the breastplate of faith and love, and for a helmet the hope of salvation. (1 Thess. 5:4–8)

When we're tired, we don't think clearly. We're groggy, and our mind is numb and slow. To be sober-minded is to be awake and alert. It's to have a sharpness to our vision.

(2) Stability of soul. The sober-minded are not easily tossed. They are steady. Listen to the cluster of terms in Titus 2:2: "Older men are to be sober-minded, dignified,

self-controlled, sound in faith, in love, and in steadfastness." If you're sober-minded, you keep your head. You don't panic. You don't over-react. There's a ballast to your boat that weathers the storms that toss the ship.

(3) Readiness to act. Sober-minded doesn't mean apathetic or passive. The sober-minded still feel deeply and rightly about reality. But because they keep their head, they act with purpose. They don't react; they respond. The apostle Peter references sober-mindedness three times in his first letter:

> Therefore, preparing your minds for action, and being sober-minded, set your hope fully on the grace that will be brought to you at the revelation of Jesus Christ. (1 Pet. 1:13)

> The end of all things is at hand; therefore be self-controlled and sober-minded for the sake of your prayers. (1 Pet. 4:7)

> Be sober-minded; be watchful. Your adversary the devil prowls around like a roaring lion, seeking someone to devour. (1 Pet. 5:8)

Poised like a sprinter at the starting line or watchful like a sheepdog on alert—to be sober-minded is to be prepared and ready to act, to pray, to fight, or to flee.

So then, to be sober-minded is to have clarity of mind, stability of soul, and readiness to act. To be sober-minded is to be mature, to have your passions governed by what is true and good and beautiful through the habitual exercise of the trained emotions.

YOU SHALL HAVE NO OTHER GODS BEFORE ME

Where does such clarity, stability, and readiness come from? We now turn to the first commandment: "You shall have no other gods before me." Or, to put it positively, "You shall love the Lord your God with all your heart, soul, mind, and strength." If Degree operates like gravity, then the triune God is the sun at the center of the solar system. It is his gravity, his weightiness, his glory that is the ballast in our boat. He is the stability of our times.

This means that we must meditate and reflect on what God is. God is a Spirit, infinite in being, glory, blessedness, and perfection; all-sufficient, eternal, unchangeable, incomprehensible, everywhere present, almighty, knowing all things, most wise, most holy, most just, most merciful and gracious, long-suffering, and abundant in goodness and truth.

This God is the maker and sustainer of all things, whose mercy is over all that he has made. He is our rock, our fortress, our refuge, our shield, and our deliverer. And he has come near to us in Jesus, who was born of the virgin Mary, suffered under Pontius Pilate, was crucified, died, was buried, descended to Hades, and on the third day rose again from the dead and ascended into heaven. Now he is seated at God's right hand, and will come again to judge the living and the dead.

This God is only available to us in Christ. His life, death and resurrection are the objective ground of our right standing before God. And this right standing—what we commonly call justification by grace alone through faith alone—is the article on which the church (and society) stands or falls. Apart from the finished work of Christ we have no hope. But Christ has reconciled sinners to a holy God, and has thereby become the stability of our souls, and the stability of our homes, and the stability of our churches, and the stability of our neighborhoods, communities, cities, states, and nations. God did not spare his own Son, but gave him up for us all, and therefore he will most assuredly give us all these things.

This then is the biblical antidote to a Crisis of Degree, the envious fever that afflicts us. The gospel of Jesus makes us right with God so that we can love him above all else. The glory of this gospel gives us gravity, so that we're sober-minded, with a clarity of mind, a stability of soul, and a readiness to act. And sober-minded leaders are able to faithfully lead their families, churches, businesses, schools, and nations through their glad-hearted and steady presence, bringing stability and life and health amidst the storms of passions that surround us.

CHAPTER 3

SABOTAGE IS COMING

THE CURE FOR OUR FEVER IS SOBER-
minded leaders who are grounded in the glory of God, and
therefore possess clarity of mind, stability of soul, and readiness to act. This enables them to orient and direct their families, churches, schools, businesses, and nations for God's
purposes. Such leaders are able to weather anxiety storms,
resist social stampedes, reject blame-shifting and excuse-
making, and maintain their integrity in an age of anxiety,
agitation, and turmoil.

But the moment that you begin to cultivate mature, sober-
minded leadership, you should expect sabotage, both from
within and without. In fact, almost like Newton's Third Law,

every act of faithful leadership will be met with an equal and opposite act of sabotage.

BEING STEERED

What do I mean by sabotage? Sabotage is any attempt to steer or derail you, to take you and your people off-mission.

The world often uses name-calling to try to steer Christians. In this case, the sabotage is overt and obvious. Biblical names for this tactic include slandering, reviling, and maligning. To resist it, we must learn how and why the tactic works.

Almost all people have a natural desire to be accepted by others. We want to be approved of, to be liked, to have a good reputation. The Bible commends a form of this desire when it says, "A good name is to be chosen rather than great riches, and favor is better than silver or gold" (Prov. 22:1). Leaders are expected to be above reproach, respectable, and "well thought of by outsiders" (1 Tim. 3:2–7).

But slander, reviling, and maligning exploit this natural desire by using insults and the threat of a bad reputation to manipulate Christians, especially Christian leaders. The world wants to turn us wherever they please, and they use slander as a steering wheel.

There are two basic kinds of steering wheels: ugly labels for true things, and ugly labels for false things. An example of the former is when Christians are called haters and bigots for condemning homosexuality. It's true that Christians condemn homosexuality. But the ugly label is meant to silence our witness by appealing to our desire for approval and acceptance and our fear of ostracism and rejection. An example of the latter is when the Pharisees called Jesus a drunkard and a glutton (which he wasn't). In this case, the world misrepresents our beliefs and then slaps an ugly label on their misrepresentation. In both cases, the purpose of the labels is to sabotage and steer us.

This tactic frequently works by exploiting the Christian desire to be a good witness to the gospel. We want our light to shine before men so that they see our good deeds and give glory to God (Matt. 5:16). Christians will often police each other in order to maintain a good testimony. The world frequently counts on this (good) Christian impulse in order to steer Christians *by means of other Christians*. Slap the ugly label on someone, and other Christians will attempt to pressure them back in line. Such pressure is frequently harder to resist, since it comes, not from the unbelieving world directly, but from the world *through* God's people.

THE SIN OF EMPATHY

The more subtle way that we're steered and sabotaged is through empathy. Now empathy, or emotion-sharing, is in itself a good and natural thing. Part of what makes us human is our ability to identify with and share the perspectives, feelings, and emotions of others. And, in fact, the Bible commands us to cultivate Christian sympathy in feeling and even to share our emotions: "Weep with those who weep, and rejoice with those who rejoice" (Rom. 12:15). As Paul says to the Corinthians, "If one member suffers, all suffer together; if one member is honored, all rejoice together" (1 Cor. 12:26). Emotion-sharing, in this sense, is an aspect of love and is designed to build connection and move us to compassionate action.

But like many good things, empathy is also dangerous. Empathy, like all passions, is meant to be governed by what is true and what is good. It's meant to be tethered to reality. But in a Crisis of Degree, empathy is often a disguise for angst and reactivity. It frequently becomes a power tool in the hands of the sensitive; it's the means by which the most immature, reactive, and invasive members of a community hijack the agenda and derail the mission. They do this by demanding that the rest of the community adapt to them and their sensitivities.

To put it more starkly, when we're under the influence of untethered empathy, we get drunk on other people's passions. In fact, that's what a social stampede is—a bunch of people who are drunk on each other's passions. Or think of the anxiety storms that rage through families, churches, and nations. Reactive passions course through a community like lightning *through the sharing of emotions*. In this sense, empathy is basically an arch-passion; it's the channel that other passions travel on between the members of a community.

Crucially, the emotions that travel between people are not always the same emotions. Sometimes one person's sadness elicits sadness in others. But at other times, sadness in one person may draw out anger in another (either at them or at the third party who is responsible for their pain). Or one person's anger awakens fear in others who go to great lengths to avoid setting them off. But the common thread is the interpersonal fusion that enables emotions to career through a community like a car with no driver. Untethered empathy puts other people's passions in the driver's seat. In such situations, appeals to empathy are frequently forms of emotional blackmail, and they often lead to cowardice, appeasement, and other failures of nerve.

The story of Aaron and the golden calf may help to make this danger more plain. In Exodus 32, Moses and Joshua are at the top of Mount Sinai, meeting with God, while Aaron and the people wait at the bottom. The people grow distressed at Moses's absence. "We don't know what happened to him," they say. Now Moses has been their leader, wielding the power of God against Pharaoh with the plagues. He stretched out his hand, and the sea parted. He struck the rock with his staff and the water flowed. When his hands were lifted up, they prevailed in battle. When his hands fell to his side, their enemies prevailed. Moses, as God's prophet, has been the living representative of God's deliverance.

His absence causes great distress and angst among the people, and so they demand that Aaron make gods to go before them, to protect them and comfort them in the face of danger. Aaron finds their distress intolerable, and concedes what should not be conceded. The strength of their emotions provokes an equally strong reaction in him. He asks for their gold and forges a golden calf. The people identify the calf as the gods who brought them out of Egypt, and Aaron builds an altar and declares a feast to Yahweh, apparently attempting to salvage some measure of faithfulness by identifying the idol with Israel's God.

This is Adamic leadership all over again. Like Adam in the garden, Aaron's abdication and failure of nerve leads to high-handed idolatry and rebellion. More than that, when Moses comes down the mountain, burning with divine anger at this great transgression, Aaron, like Adam, shifts the blame:

> "You know the people, that they are set on evil. For they said to me, 'Make us gods who shall go before us. As for this Moses, the man who brought us up out of the land of Egypt, we do not know what has become of him.' So I said to them, 'Let any who have gold take it off.' So they gave it to me, and I threw it into the fire, and out came this calf." (Exod. 32:22–24)

"The people you gave me did it. I was just standing here, minding my own business, and out popped this calf." Abdication, Idolatry, and Blame-shifting. Same song, new verse. The people break loose because Aaron, their leader, let them break loose, to the derision of their enemies (Exod. 32:25).

The same pattern appears in 1 Samuel 15. The Lord gives King Saul a mission through the prophet Samuel—to strike the Amalekites because they had harassed Israel when they were weak. Everything is to be devoted to destruction, both the people and the livestock. Nothing is to be spared. This is holy divine judgment against the Amalekites, with Saul and the Israelites playing the role of the angel of death.

But Saul spares King Agag of the Amalekites, as well as the best of livestock, and only devotes the worthless ones to destruction. When Samuel arrives, Saul says, "I have performed the commandment of the Lord." Samuel responds, "What then is this bleating of the sheep in my ears and the lowing of the oxen that I hear?" Saul is ready with an answer: "They have brought them from the Amalekites, for the people spared the best of the sheep and of the oxen to sacrifice to the LORD your God, and the rest we have devoted to destruction" (1 Sam. 15:13-15).

Samuel reminds Saul that God anointed him as king over Israel—he's the head and responsible for the people—and God gave him a very specific mission: "Go, devote to destruction the sinners, the Amalekites, and fight against them until they are consumed" (1 Sam. 15:18). Instead, Saul has disobeyed the Lord and pounced on the spoil.

But Saul has not finished with the excuses.

> "I have obeyed the voice of the LORD. I have gone on the mission on which the LORD sent me. I have brought Agag the king of Amalek, and I have devoted the Amalekites to destruction. But the people took of the spoil, sheep and oxen, the best of the things devoted to destruction, to sacrifice to the LORD your God in Gilgal." (1 Sam. 15:20-21)

Samuel will have none of it. The Lord wants obedience, not sacrifice. This sort of rebellion is as bad as divination. This sort of presumption is just as wicked as idolatry, and God has rejected Saul as king. Saul finally confesses: "I have sinned, for I have transgressed the commandment of the Lord and your words, because I feared the people and obeyed their voice" (1 Sam. 15:24). Like with Adam and Aaron: Abdication, Idolatry, and Blame-shifting.

STRENGTHENING OUR NERVE

So then, in the face of sabotage, how do we grow in our ability to wisely and faithfully resist being steered, both by slander and by emotion-sharing?

First, take responsibility for yourself, your emotions, and your actions. Don't shift the blame. That's what maturity fundamentally is—taking responsibility for oneself. The immature are tossed about by winds of doctrine and storms of passion, and they always have an excuse. But mature leaders are steady, stable, and take responsibility for themselves.

This means getting clear on the nature of responsibility. The world operates according to a zero-sum notion of responsibility. If one person is 100% responsible, then everyone else must have zero responsibility. If one person's responsibility increases, then everyone else's must necessarily decrease by the same amount. Such a mentality fuels blame-shifting, since we believe that the sin of other people excuses our own. But this is false. We are not guilty for the sins of other people. But neither do their sins excuse ours. While other people may influence us, ultimately, we are responsible for ourselves and what God has entrusted to us.

Second, know yourself. Grow in self-awareness. Pay attention to your passions—your reluctances, hesitations, anxieties, frustrations, moods, and snap reactions. What makes you flinch? When do you walk on eggshells? What topics are off-limits? Who do you avoid offending? When do you blow up and escalate? When do you shrink back and shut down?

To bring it back to the sabotage of slander: What label makes you flinch? What names will you go to great lengths to avoid being called? And don't limit yourself to obvious ones like "bigot." Because steering labels vary by context, we must learn to be alert to the more subtle ones. "Racist," "woke," "Christian nationalist," "fundamentalist," "right-wing," "left-wing, "coward," "quarrelsome," "compromiser"—any of these (and more) can become steering labels, depending on the community whose approval we seek.

Our passions are not always trustworthy, but they are always telling us something. Self-awareness allows us to interrogate them, to see whether they are well-founded and tethered to reality, and to resist them when they are not. It also allows us to gain the necessary emotional distance so that we can act wisely, and perhaps seek extra counsel when we're amped up or weighed down. C.S. Lewis taught us that the surest way to disarm anger or lust is to turn our attention away from the girl or the insult and to start examining the passion itself. Thus, we must grow in our self-awareness and have the strength of mind to step out of the stream of passions and reactions in order to rightly examine them.

This sort of self-awareness is not merely a human skill. It's a divine gift, and we ought to ask God for it. David prays, "Search me, O God, and know my heart! Try me and know my thoughts! And see if there be any grievous way in me, and lead me in the way everlasting!" (Ps. 139:23–24). God is the one who tests our hearts and minds. He discerns our anxious thoughts, our fears and cares, our passions and our moods. More than that, he exposes the rationalizations and excuses that we often use to hide them.

Third, calibrate your standards by the word of God. How does God define "a grievous way"? What offends him? We must define sin the way the Bible does, and not the way that the world does. The world will frequently seek to co-opt God's standards by maximizing their offense at certain sins while completely ignoring other ones. It takes spiritual effort to resist adopting such selective, worldly standards. It requires us to be transformed by the renewal of our minds (Rom. 12:2). So when you're called a nasty name, ask whether God regards the substance of that name as sinful, and be alert lest you begin to internally flinch at things that the Bible teaches.

But it's not enough to calibrate our standards; we also need to calibrate our loves and hates. First and foremost, we must love and treasure God above all things. No other gods before him. And this means that we must love what God loves and hate what God hates. There is a crucial affectional dimension to our resistance. Our emotions and passions have to be brought to heel, trained to value what is valuable, to abhor what is evil, and to fear the Lord (and not men).

Fourth, increase your own tolerance for emotional pain and distress. Aaron could not bear the agitation of the Hebrews. Saul feared the people. If we have a low threshold for emotional pain, we will seek a quick (and often short-term) fix. Anything to relieve the immediate discomfort. Sober-minded leaders, on the other hand, have stamina and endurance, because they are able to retain a healthy emotional distance while remaining connected to those in their care. Rather than channeling the reactive passions in the system, they are shock absorbers who know that crises often cannot be fixed, but instead must be endured. They begin with sober-minded stability, and therefore are free to be wisely compassionate. They can rightly weep with those who weep, because they are tethered to Christ.

Fifth, be willing to be called ugly names. More than that, *rejoice* when you are slandered. As Jesus says in the Sermon on the Mount, "Blessed are you when others revile you and persecute you and utter all kinds of evil against you falsely on my account. Rejoice and be glad, for your reward is great in heaven, for so they persecuted the prophets who were before you" (Matt. 5:11–12). In other words, we rejoice when slandered because we are in good company. As Jesus says elsewhere, "If they have called the master of the house Beelzebul, how much more will they malign those of his household" (Matt. 10:25). If they said Jesus was demonic, don't be surprised when they say you are too.

Sixth, make sure the slanders are actually false. When you are slandered, one temptation is to lean into the lie until it becomes true. "If I'm going to be hanged as a thief, I might as well steal something." But notice that this is simply another form of being steered. It's reactive. There's no virtue in becoming the ungodly thing that your enemies think you already are.

Paul exhorts Christians to adorn the doctrine of our God and Savior (Titus 2:10), and to do what we can, within reason, to avoid giving our adversaries occasion for slander (1 Tim. 5:14). Evil men may utter falsehoods about us, but we ought not supply them with excess ammunition through our own foolish, immature, and reactive behavior. This is especially true of pastors and other Christian leaders, who should aim to be "well thought of by outsiders" (1 Tim. 3:7).

Seventh, when you are slandered, resolve not to respond in kind. Christ is our model, and Peter exhorts us to follow in his steps. "When he was reviled, he did not revile in return; when he suffered, he did not threaten, but continued entrusting himself to him who judges justly" (1 Pet. 2:23). Doing so requires us to distinguish between holy mockery of sin and rebellion (which is lawful) and reactive derision flowing from contempt, anger, and other ungodly passions. Holy mockery seeks to edify others by exposing rebellion for the folly that it is. It is deliberate and purposeful, not reactive, and aims to both honor God and love others.

Finally, root all of your resistance to sabotage in a sincere and honest desire to please God. When Paul is slandered by the Judaizers, he is unmoved because he has a clean conscience and knows whose approval he seeks: "For am I now seeking the approval of man, or of God? Or am I trying to please man? If I were still trying to please man, I would not be a servant of Christ" (Gal. 1:10).

Elsewhere he says, "For our appeal does not spring from error or impurity or any attempt to deceive, but just as we have been approved by God to be entrusted with the gospel, so we speak, not to please man, but to please God who tests our hearts" (1 Thess. 2:3–4). Paul welcomes God's testing and therefore can resist the pull of man-pleasing and man-fearing.

The apostle Peter devotes much of his first letter to building his reader's resistance to being steered. He knows that the world will "speak against us as evildoers" (1 Pet. 2:12). They will malign us because we refuse to join them in their debauchery (1 Pet. 4:4). Therefore, we shouldn't be surprised by such trials and insults (1 Pet. 4:12–14).

Echoing the words of Christ, Peter writes,

> But even if you should suffer for righteousness' sake, you will be blessed. Have no fear of them, nor be troubled, but in your hearts honor Christ the Lord as holy, always being prepared to make a defense to anyone who asks you for a reason for the hope that is in you; yet do it with gentleness and respect, having a good conscience, so that, when you are slandered, those who revile your good behavior in Christ may be put to shame. (1 Pet. 3:14–16)

Honoring Christ as the Holy One enables us to endure reviling and slander, because our conscience is clear and God has promised us his blessing when we suffer for righteousness' sake.

Sabotage is inevitable. Attempts to steer you will come. The world will seek to wield names and labels against you in order to manipulate and render you mute and impotent. You will be tempted to let your own passions and the passions of others sweep you off your feet. Your hands will grow weak, your knees will grow feeble, and your nerve will begin to fail. But by God's grace, you can resist the lure of people-pleasing and man-fearing. You can know yourself, take responsibility for yourself, and calibrate your standards and your loves. With God's help, you can be steadfast and immovable, grounded in the gospel of our happy God as you seek his approval above all else.

CHAPTER 4

COURAGE IN THE HOME

SO THEN, IF WE ARE LIVING IN THE MIDST of cultural chaos and social disintegration, and if sober-minded leadership rooted in the gospel is the solution, what does this look like in practice? These final three chapters will explore faithful leadership in the home, the church, and the world.

We begin in the home, because it is the proving ground for everything else. You can't export what you don't have. One of the central requirements for leadership in the church is that a man manage his household well (1 Tim. 3:5). If you can't lead your own house, how can you possibly lead God's house? If your kids are out of control, how can you expect to faithfully lead the people of God? And while this principle is a clear biblical qualification for leadership in the church, it can also be wisely applied in other areas such as business and politics, since it is simply an application of the more general biblical truth that before you can be set over much, you must first be faithful in little (Matt. 25:21).

So then, what does mature, sober-minded leadership look like in the home? We'll explore this question through the household code of Ephesians chapters 5 and 6. In this passage, Paul displays what faithful headship looks like in the Christian family.

> Wives, submit to your own husbands, as to the Lord. For the husband is the head of the wife even as Christ is the head of the church, his body, and is himself its Savior. Now as the church submits to Christ, so also wives should submit in everything to their husbands.
>
> Husbands, love your wives, as Christ loved the church and gave himself up for her, that he might sanctify her, having cleansed her by the washing of water with the word, so that he might present the church to himself in splendor, without spot or wrinkle or any such thing, that she might be holy and without blemish. In the same way husbands should love their wives as their own bodies. He who loves his wife loves himself. For no one ever hated his own flesh, but nourishes and cherishes it, just as Christ does the church, because we are members of his body. "Therefore a man shall leave his father and mother and hold fast to his wife, and the two shall become one flesh." This mystery is profound, and

I am saying that it refers to Christ and the church. However, let each one of you love his wife as himself, and let the wife see that she respects her husband.

Children, obey your parents in the Lord, for this is right. "Honor your father and mother" (this is the first commandment with a promise), "that it may go well with you and that you may live long in the land." Fathers, do not provoke your children to anger, but bring them up in the discipline and instruction of the Lord. (Eph. 5:22–6:4)

The headship of the husband is a fact, not a command. The Bible does not teach that a husband *ought* to be the head of his wife and his household. It teaches that he *is* the head of his household, whether he wants to be or not. Male headship is a given. It may be a domineering headship. It may be an absentee headship. It may be a strong, sacrificial headship. But one way or another, the husband is the head. Period. The only question is whether he will be an unfaithful head like Adam, or a faithful head like Christ.

TAKING RESPONSIBILITY

What does faithful headship look like? First, faithful headship means that you are responsible for the whole body. All of it. It means that you must know God's purpose for your household, and you must take initiative to put your house in order for the sake of God's purposes.

A mature husband wakes up in the morning knowing who he is and what he's about. More than that, he knows what his household is for, and seeks to set his family up for fruitfulness and success. A friend of mine accomplishes this through a weekly meeting with his wife in order to get clarity on the upcoming week, and to seek her help in carrying out the household mission. He initiates and sets the general direction ("Here are the activities and projects we want to prioritize this week"), and then seeks her feedback to fine-tune the focus ("Don't forget that we need to clean out the guest bedroom before company arrives next weekend"), and then seeks to provide what she needs in order to make the mission fruitful ("I'll be sure to be home from work early on Wednesday to get everything ready for their arrival").

Now the household is the basic unit of society, established by God for the sake of fruitful growth and faithful stewardship of God's world. God has called Man to be fruitful, multiply, fill the earth and subdue it, exercising dominion over its inhabitants. And the household is the first and primary place where we fulfill this calling. As the head, you are responsible to lead and guide your household for this purpose, to organize it for the sake of God's mission, and to provide the spiritual, emotional, and material resources that your family needs to fulfill their calling. This includes everything from your own personal piety and prayers to financial provision, from your time and attention to your affection and active presence.

Again, you are responsible for the whole, even as the other members of your household are responsible for their God-given tasks. This means that you are responsible for your household's sins, even if you're not personally to blame for them. When God called the first household to account for their rebellion, he approached Adam first. Though Eve was the first to eat from the forbidden tree, God sought out Adam first: "Where are you [singular]?" As the head, Adam was responsible for the whole thing, even as Eve was to blame for her actions and particular consequences fell upon each of them individually.

The same truth is illustrated in Aaron at Mount Sinai. Even though the people had initiated the idolatry, Moses addresses Aaron directly: "What did this people do to you that you have brought such a great sin upon them?" (Exod. 32:21). Or again, when Samuel confronts King Saul over the Amalekites, he will not allow Saul to evade responsibility by blaming the people. God anointed Saul as king, as head of the people. God gave Saul the mission. Saul was therefore responsible for ensuring the obedience of the whole body, even if he wasn't personally to blame for every transgression.

Faithful headship therefore means that you must reject all blame-shifting and excuse-making. Your wife's sin is never an excuse for your failures. Your kids' sin is never an excuse for your sin. You cannot say, "The woman you gave me." You cannot say, "You know the children, how their hearts are set on evil." You cannot say, "I feared my family, and listened to their voice." Instead, step up to the plate and take responsibility, first for yourself and then for your family. Remember that Job is commended for offering sacrifices on behalf of his children, simply because they might have sinned and cursed God in their hearts (Job 1:5). As a righteous father, he knew his responsibility before God.

DOING THE HARD THING, NOT THE EASY THING

Second, faithful headship sacrifices for the good of the body and the mission. We see this in Paul's particular command to husbands. Love your wife as your own body. Love your wife the way that Christ loves the church, nourishing and cherishing her, giving himself for her that she might be holy and glorious.

It's crucial that we get clear on what this sacrificial giving entails. In this context, to sacrifice is to do the hard costly thing that pleases God—and not necessarily your wife or your kids. They are not God. We must not subscribe to the "If Mama Ain't Happy Ain't Nobody Happy" School of Husbanding. That turns headship on its head. There will be a great temptation to do so, and to rationalize it by appealing to sacrificial service. But catering and acquiescing to one's wife is often the easy way out; the hard and costly thing would be to lean in, to engage, to have difficult conversations and seek to come to one mind.

This means, at times, a husband must be willing to endure his wife's displeasure in order to fulfill his calling as the head of his household. Because this principle is easily abused by fools and petty tyrants, it must be applied with wisdom and humility. A faithful husband will seek wise counsel from his pastor and from other godly men in evaluating whether he is showing godly fortitude or stubborn folly. The story of Nabal is in the Bible for a reason. In fact, that story underscores how important it is for a wise husband to welcome the wisdom and accept the correction of a godly wife. But he must not make her approval the standard. As Doug Wilson says, a man who cannot stand up to his wife will never be able to stand up for his wife.

SETTING THE TEMPERATURE OF STEADY JOY

Third, faithful headship cultivates an atmosphere of joy in Christ and gratitude to God in his home. This is implied in the second major command in the Ephesians passage: raise your children in the discipline and instruction of the Lord, refusing to provoke, exasperate, or frustrate them. The *paideia* of the Lord is a glad and glorious thing. It is not dour or sullen or anxious or frustrated. It is life and joy and gratitude to God for all of his kindness.

A faithful husband, then, is alert to the spiritual temperature of his home. And he's not merely a thermometer; he's a thermostat. He sets the tone in his home, first through his own glad-hearted, steady, and grateful presence, and then through concrete words and deeds.

In doing so, he displays all three dimensions of sober-mindedness: clarity of mind, stability of soul, and readiness to act.

Clarity of mind. He is sensitive to any crackle in the air, to the presence of poisonous passions among his household, such as bitterness, grumbling, complaining, and disrespect. In particular, he is alert to the presence or absence of playfulness in his household. Playfulness is a key indicator of trust, love, security, and health. Its absence is a sign that sinful passions are boiling beneath the surface. The family that plays together stays together.

Stability of soul. He is able to step out of the cycle of reactive passions, acting as an anchor for his family in the midst of anxiety storms, receiving emotional lightning strikes from his wife and children without amplifying them or passing them along. When things go wrong, he doesn't get defensive, nor does he abdicate. His heart remains firm and steady, trusting in the Lord.

Readiness to act. Because he sees clearly and remains steady, he is able to act wisely, stepping into conflicts with curiosity, compassion, and courage. He sees conflict as an opportunity for discipleship. He avoids unnecessary escalation, instead applying faithful and steady pressure with wisdom and grace.

GET CURIOUS AND REFRAME CONFLICT

Practically speaking, this means that a sober-minded husband and father knows how to remember the right things and ask the right questions. His sober-mindedness enables his curiosity, which is an often unrecognized aspect of love. The apostle Peter exhorts husbands to "live with their wives in an understanding way" (1 Pet. 3:7). This means that a husband has the wherewithal to remember what he knows about his wife in the heat of the moment. It also means he acknowledges when he doesn't understand his wife, and then seeks the knowledge necessary to love her well. When his wife reacts harshly or negatively to something he says, rather than being personally offended and escalating the conflict, he tries to better understand where the reaction came from. What am I missing? Why did she react that way? What was underneath it?

Such curiosity is the prerequisite to compassion. Psalm 103:13–14 teaches us that "as a father shows compassion to his children, so the LORD shows compassion to those who fear him. For he knows our frame; he remembers that we are dust." Notice that the Lord's compassion is likened to a father's compassion. And then notice that God's compassion is tied to his knowledge of our frame; he remembers that we are dust. You also must know your children's frame, and tailor your compassion to who they are. But unlike God, who simply knows it, you must learn it. You must get curious.

Not only does sober-mindedness enable curiosity and compassion, it also enables us to reframe and reorient conflict. For example, say that a newly married husband and wife are in the midst of a car-gument, those frequently frustrating disagreements on the way home from a dinner party. A wise husband is alert to the ways that he and his wife begin to view each other as "the problem," pushing and pressing and escalating the conflict by approaching it as adversaries. Such antagonism builds a wall between the two of them, one that has the potential to long outlast this particular fight. When he detects this, his first task is to step outside their mutual passions and heed the words of President Reagan to "tear down that wall." Instead of viewing each other as the problem, he must lead them in viewing the *problem* as the problem, and the two of them as collaborators in addressing it.

This sort of maturity echoes beyond the immediate family to one's extended family. In my premarital counseling, I often spend a significant portion of time talking to engaged couples about their respective families of origin, encouraging them to get curious about how they relate to their parents and siblings as a way of preparing for marriage. Their families have inevitably shaped their habits and patterns (for good and for ill). And frequently there are patterns of reactivity that feel normal to one person, but which will shock the other when he or she encounters them. In fact, the new spouse is often the occasion for exposing the ways that we have appeased, coped with, and managed family conflict and sin.

When such tangles emerge, whether in the husband's family or the wife's, the burden is on the husband to patiently and carefully address them. In doing so, his first goal must be to establish his own household in the Lord. When he gets married, a man leaves his father and mother and cleaves to his wife. Such leaving and cleaving is often more difficult than we expect, as patterns forged over decades collide with the new covenantal reality. Under God, a husband's fundamental allegiance is now to his wife, and hers to him. Together, they form the nucleus of a new household whose goal is not to personally alter the habits of their in-laws, but instead to maintain the integrity of their new home in the face of sabotage, guilt trips, and other forms of family drama.

THE TOOLBELT

One of the key indicators of mature and healthy headship is the ability to bring a wide array of responses to bear in a given situation. An immature man simply reacts. Disrespect from his kids triggers anger. A challenge from his wife causes him to shut down. But a sober-minded leader aims to cultivate the discipline and instruction of the Lord in his home by using all the tools in his tool belt, beginning with his words.

A godly father *instructs and teaches,* proactively imparting wisdom to prepare his family for the challenges of life. Instruction aims to build up a reservoir of practical training about what our families need to *believe,* and what they need to *do.* We teach and train in formal ways (catechisms, Bible reading, and family devotions) and in informal ways (applying the word "as we go," as Deuteronomy 6 tells us).

A godly father *warns and admonishes,* anticipating particular dangers and temptations and offering both wake-up calls and wise counsel. While instruction highlights more general duties, admonition targets specific temptations that are present in the moment. Such warnings frequently flow from our authority and experience, and often make use of cautionary tales to spur those in our care away from sin. A mature father doesn't begrudge the fact that he must give the same warnings over and over; the repetition is the point.

A godly father *corrects and rebukes,* expressing appropriate disapproval and redirecting members of his household from continuing in sin. Whereas warnings address our families as they confront temptations, rebuke speaks to them when they have begun to travel down a sinful path. Rebuke and correction must be sharp but gentle, flowing from genuine affection and not from reactive anger and frustration. The most common pitfall when correcting is for strong disapproval to become harsh and bitter. Fathers must not exasperate their children (Eph. 6:4; Col. 3:21), and one of the surest ways to provoke them is to be provoked by them. The gentleness that is essential to godly correction flows from sober-minded steadiness that governs our own passions as we seek to shepherd those of our children.

A godly father *rewards and disciplines*, praising what is good and providing painful consequences for what is evil in hopes of drawing his people back to the Lord. When children are young, such consequences are typically artificial (such as spanking). As they grow up, a godly father often allows natural consequences to fall on his children's heads so that they learn from experience. In either case, discipline is like a corrective mini-judgment designed to keep our kids from being exposed to more substantial judgment. Praise, on the other hand, is just as important, and flows from both a baseline delight (because your kids are yours) and a specific delight (because their particular actions are pleasing).

A godly father *commands and exhorts*, giving clear expectations based on his authority and coming alongside to encourage his family in the path of righteousness. Commands rely directly on parental authority, such that "because I said so" is a sufficient reason to expect obedience. In general, commands ought to be used sparingly, and only when you are prepared to follow through should defiance arise. On the other hand, exhortation is more of a call to shared obedience. It takes the form of "Let us" versus "You must." Exhortations are encouraging spurs designed to give fortitude and perseverance in the face of temptations and obstacles to obedience.

FIRST IN, LAST OUT, LAUGHING LOUDEST

Not only does a mature husband and father use appropriate words for each occasion, he also leads with his deeds. One of my favorite descriptions of godly headship is given by King Lune of Archenland in *The Horse and His Boy*.

> "For this is what it means to be a king: to be first in every desperate attack and last in every desperate retreat, and when there's hunger in the land (as must be now and then in bad years) to wear finer clothes and laugh louder over a scantier meal than any man in your land."[1]

Faithful kingship (or headship) means leading from both the front and the back. If there's a danger to be faced, the head will face it first. If there's a burden to be borne, the head will bear it first. A man will see to it that pain and hardship fall in his lap before they ever fall upon those under his care. And he will bear the pain the longest. He will be last in every desperate retreat. He will ensure the safety and security of others before securing his own. And he will do so with great joy. His attitude is the same as the apostle Paul, who wrote, "I will most gladly spend and be spent for your souls" (2 Cor. 12:15). Yes, there are sacrifices. Yes, there are hardships. Yes, there are scanty meals and confusing trials and frustrating seasons. We save ourselves up and then pour ourselves out. And we do so with a twinkle in our eye and laughter in our bones.

Practically this means that a godly husband will come home not to be served, but to serve. After a hard day's work, a godly man enters his home, not with a list of demands, but with an eagerness to give. He comes to relieve

1. C. S. Lewis, *The Horse and His Boy* (New York: HarperCollins, 1994), 223.

the burdens of his wife, not add to them. He comes to play with his kids, not shunt them off to their rooms while he puts his feet up.

In particular, a faithful husband and father recognizes the importance of his presence, his time, and his affection. His aim is to be the smile of God to his wife and his family, to embody for them the gospel of the glory of the happy God. This means a regular diet of tickle fights, wrestling matches, reassuring hugs, intentional conversations, and all of it shot through with the joy of the Lord.

THE SUN, THE BRIDEGROOM, AND THE WARRIOR

All of us, as husbands and fathers, need regular reminders to help us fulfill our calling as heads of our households. And thankfully, God's word directs us to a daily and unavoidable reminder of what it means to be a godly man. We find it in Psalm 19:

> In them [the heavens] he has set a tent for the sun,
> which comes out like a bridegroom leaving his chamber,
> and, like a strong man, runs its course with joy. (Ps. 19:4–5)

The sun, as it moves across the sky, reminds David of something. He's seen that brightness before. Then he recalls the wedding day of a close friend, and the link is made—the sun is like the bridegroom.

These days, when the wedding march begins, all eyes turn to the back of the room to see the bride, clothed in white and beautiful in her glory. But a wise attendee will also steal a glance toward the altar, where the groom waits with eager anticipation and expectant joy. The beauty of his bride is reflected in the brightness of his face. It's that look that David remembers when he sees the sun rise in the morning.

But David doesn't stop there. David considers the sun again and is reminded of a warrior, a *gibborim*, one of his mighty men, running into battle with spear raised and eyes blazing because he is doing what he was built to do (2 Sam. 23:8). The warrior is intense and joyful because he is protecting his people with the strength and skill that God has given him.

So then, the sun is like the groom, and the sun is like the mighty man. Both are images of godly masculinity—the bridegroom and the warrior, the lover and the man of war. Both images direct us to a man's calling in relation to his people. One points us inward, as a man delights in his wife (and by extension his children). The other points us outward, as a man protects his people from external threats, whether physical or spiritual. The sun, then, is an ever-present reminder of what it means to be a godly man: bright, triumphant, blazing with joy and purpose, ready to fight and bleed and die for the ones he loves.

GRAVITY AND GLADNESS

By linking the sun to the bridegroom and the warrior, David gives us an image of gravity. *Gravitas*, or the weight of a man's presence, is at the heart of mature masculinity. It's the dignity and honor and stability that pulls people into your orbit, like the sun that orients the planets by its mass. It comes partly from a man's skill and competence, partly from his sober-mindedness and confidence, but ultimately from his fear of the Lord. The fear of the Lord gives weight to a man's soul, making him firm and stable and steadfast, not tossed to and fro by winds of doctrine or the passions of the flesh.

But as Psalm 19 shows, gravitas is only one half of the equation. Gladness completes the picture. It's not enough to take initiative and responsibility for oneself and for others. A godly man runs his course *with joy*. Competence, confidence, strength, and sacrifice are all essential to faithful headship. But joy crowns all. Faithful headship leads and bleeds and sacrifices with unconquerable joy. First in, last out, laughing loudest.

Psalm 19 presents the sun as a wonderful picture of true masculinity. But for David, the sun doesn't merely draw our minds to the bridegroom and the strong man, to the lover and the man of war. More than that, the sun draws our minds upward to the splendor and majesty of the Maker. "The heavens declare the glory *of God*" (Ps. 19:1). The sun both reminds us of the glory of manhood and displays the glory of our Creator.

More than that, these reminders point us to Christ. He is the ground and goal of manhood. All true gravity and gladness come from him. He is the one who reconciles us to God so that, despite our sin and shame, we live beneath the smile of a happy Father, one who says to us, "This is my beloved son, with whom I am well pleased" (Matt. 3:17).

Jesus is our older brother, the firstborn from the dead, our model and example who ran his race for the joy set before him. He is the ultimate strong man—a man of war who killed the dragon to get the girl. He is the bridegroom who greatly rejoices over his bride and whose face is like the sun shining in full strength. And every day, he causes the sun to rise, reminding us of who he is and who we are to be.

CHAPTER 5

COURAGE IN THE CHURCH

WE MOVE NOW FROM THE HOUSEHOLD TO the church. What does sober-minded leadership look like among God's people, especially in the midst of conflict? While the focus of this chapter will be on the church proper, the principles are applicable to any type of Christian organization, whether a school or a business or a ministry. We'll take as our case study the confrontation at Antioch, recorded by Paul in Galatians 2.

> But when Cephas came to Antioch, I opposed him to his face, because he stood condemned. For before certain men came from James, he was eating with the Gentiles; but when

they came he drew back and separated himself, fearing the circumcision party. And the rest of the Jews acted hypocritically along with him, so that even Barnabas was led astray by their hypocrisy. But when I saw that their conduct was not in step with the truth of the gospel, I said to Cephas before them all, "If you, though a Jew, live like a Gentile and not like a Jew, how can you force the Gentiles to live like Jews?" (Gal. 2:11–14)

JEWS, GENTILES, AND EVERYONE IN BETWEEN

To understand this passage, we have to understand the wider religious context in the first century. For Jews at this time, the fundamental division in the world was between Jews and Gentiles, those in the covenant and those outside. This division dated back to Genesis 12 when God made a covenant with Abram. But of course, the division was never quite that simple. There were other people descended from Abraham (Ishmaelites and Edomites), or other splinter groups (like Samaritans). In the book of Acts, we know that there were groups of God-fearers, Gentiles who worshiped Israel's God, but did not fully adopt the Jewish law, especially food laws and circumcision. And within Judaism itself, there were various sectarian groups: Pharisees, Sadducees, Herodians, Essenes, and so forth. But still the basic division was Jew and Gentile.

Into that world comes the gospel, the good news that Jesus is the Messiah, Israel's king, and indeed the Son of

God—and that through his death and resurrection, he rescues both Jews and Gentiles from sin and death. This good news scrambles that basic division. As a result, the social picture in the first century is complex and confusing. Here is a sampling of the various groups in play.

First, you have unbelieving Gentiles, pagans and idolaters of various kinds.

Next, you have unbelieving Jews, divided into various parties and groups. One group of unbelieving Jews was particularly zealous for the Jewish law and its traditions. This group often expressed that zeal by persecuting other less zealous Jews. This is the group that would have led the persecution against the early Christians, whom they regarded as unfaithful to the traditions of the fathers. And as Paul notes in Galatians 1, this is the group that he was once a part of.

Then you have the early Christians. But there were various groups that claimed that name. There were Jewish "Christians" who preached Jesus + Torah, Jesus + Keeping the Jewish law, including circumcision and food laws, and expected Gentile Christians to do the same. This was the Law-observant and Law-preaching mission to the Gentiles. And we can call this group the Agitators or Troublers, since they are the ones that Paul says were troubling the Galatians. Then there were Jewish Christians who continued to practice Jewish customs themselves but did not require Gentiles to do so. Some, like Paul, only did so when engaged in evangelism to Jews (1 Cor. 9, Acts 22). Others likely did so out of habit and custom all the time. Then there were Gentile Christians, some who simply trusted in Jesus for deliverance from sin and death without adopting circumcision and so forth, and others who trusted in Jesus and sought to keep the whole Law, including circumcision and food laws, usually under pressure from the Troublers.

THE SITUATION IN GALATIA

That's the wider social context. In this particular passage, a number of different groups and individuals are mentioned. First, you have the circumcision party (either unbelieving Jews who were persecuting Christians in Jerusalem, or perhaps the Troublers, the Jesus + circumcision "Christians"). You have James and the Jerusalem apostles (who had previously not compelled Gentiles like Titus to be circumcised; see Galatians 2:3). You have the men from James who come to Peter with a message. Then there's Peter, the rest of the Jews, Barnabas, the Gentile Christians, and last of all, Paul.

This is a highly combustible situation, filled with the potential for social stampedes and scapegoating—just read the early chapters of the book of Acts. There have already been persecutions in Jerusalem in response to the preaching of the apostles and the inclusion of the Gentiles.

With that background, let's reconstruct the particular situation in Galatians 2. Up to this point, Peter has been regularly sharing table fellowship with Gentiles. Then something happens and James sends some men to Peter with a message. We're not told exactly what it said, but it probably went something like this: "Peter, dining with the Gentiles is creating problems for us. We're under a lot of pressure here. The circumcision party is stirring things up. People are being hauled before the Sanhedrin, getting kicked out of the synagogues. It's rough. And people have heard that you're eating with uncircumcised Gentiles. So for the moment, could you turn the heat down for us? Maybe don't eat with them for a while? Just until things cool off." We don't have to assume that James and Peter have completely rejected the gospel. In fact, it's clear that they haven't, since their actions are described as hypocrisy—believing one thing, but behaving in a different way. Instead, it's more likely that the appeal was about wisdom and prudence, about fear of the circumcision party and compassion for those being persecuted.

But whatever the specific message was, it changes Peter's behavior. He draws back and separates himself from the Gentiles. And the rest of the Jews, including Barnabas, join him in his hypocritical separation.

HOW PRESSURE WORKS

What can we learn from this failure of leadership?

First, note how the pressure works. It begins far away, with zealous unbelieving Jews. The pressure then moves in, running from the Troublers to James through his messengers to Peter, and then from Peter to the rest of the Jews and Barnabas.

This is frequently how pressure works in Christian communities. The world puts pressure on Christians to act in a certain way. As a faithful Christian, you don't care what the world thinks; that pressure doesn't hit you directly. But

Christian A cares. But you don't care what Christian A thinks, because you think he's compromised. But Christian B cares what Christian A thinks. But you don't care about Christian B either; he's not in your community. But Christian C cares what Christian B thinks, and Christian C is a pastor in your denomination, an elder on your council, a respected member of your community, a close friend. And now he is channeling and amplifying the worldly pressure directly to you.

This is an important principle: the greatest pressure comes from those closest to you. This of course is not a bad thing. It's a good and glorious thing. You ought to care what your fellow pastors think, or what respected members of your community think. You ought to desire their wisdom. Humility demands that you look at yourself with sober judgment and receive counsel from other godly leaders. But you ought to also be alert to the way that this good gift can be hijacked and used to trouble and derail your church, your school, and your community.

To connect this chapter to the last one, sometimes the greatest pressure in an elder meeting originates in a fellow elder's household. He channels the world's angst and agitation into the meeting, because his wife is channeling it into his home. You can begin to predict a pastor's sermon application on Sunday by reading his wife's Facebook page on Friday.

So then, how can you tell the difference between the wrong kind of pressure and the right kind? One key test is whether you can name the issue. Can you talk about the elephant in the room? Or is the pressure always subtle, always masked, always out of direct view? In your discussions, are you seeking to persuade each other about what's good and wise, or are you seeking to pressure and manipulate each other to avoid conflict?

This underscores that the kind of sensitivity leaders need is a sensitivity to their own passions and reactions. We must be able to name the pressure, to identify its source, to see how it travels in our community, and how it justifies itself. Recent years have provided ample opportunities to examine these dynamics. Think of the controversies in the church over COVID restrictions, over the COVID vaccine, over race, gender, and sexuality, over political philosophy and cultural engagement. Each of these careened through congregations and schools, provoking reactions and magnifying divisions. The particulars may have varied, but the reactive dynamics were the same, as worldly pressures were laundered through Christian rhetoric and brought to bear on Christian leaders around the country.

SLANDER, RESPECTABILITY, AND THE DANGER OF WINSOMENESS

Second, note how the pressure in Galatians was about separating from some group of undesirable Christians. In the first century, it was uncircumcised Gentiles. Who is it today? More importantly, who is it for your community? Because again, the particular pressures will differ from community to community. There will be pressure not to read that author, or listen to that podcast, or attend that conference, or be a part of that church, or associate with those people.

As we saw in a previous chapter, slander is often an effective weapon in creating this pressure, preying on our fear of man and desire for their approval—these sins are two sides of the same coin. And we must recognize that the true target of the slander is often not who we think. We think that the one slandered is the target. But the true target is that guy's friends. The goal is to make the slandered one so toxic that others simply sidle away from him, putting a respectable distance of deniability between them.

To tie in the previous principle, the world will often slander others in order to steer you by your soft-hearted friends. Christian C puts pressure on you to avoid associating with Christian D because of what the world and Christian A and Christian B think. These sorts of accusations are designed to create a fog around a person in hopes that people will say, "Where there's smoke, there's fire. Mark and avoid." Never mind the smoke machine that is actually creating the fog. In other words, people will attempt to steer us through guilt by association: "If we don't separate from this group of undesirables, then everybody else will separate from us."

And so the question we must ask ourselves as leaders is this. Do we allow other people to choose our friends, to define the boundaries of our fellowship? Or does Christ define those boundaries?

Of course, there are times when we must separate, when we must avoid fellowship with those who profess to be brothers but deny it by their high-handed sin. There are times when we must remove leaven from our midst, and "purge the evil person from among us" (1 Cor. 5:9–13). What's more, there are times when we might choose to part ways amicably because of differences in ministry philosophy. In Galatians 2, Paul was on a mission to the uncircumcised, while the Jerusalem apostles focused on the circumcised. The mission fields were different, and so they separated, but they still extended to one another the right hand of fellowship.

But even here, there is a danger lurking. It's tempting to separate from fellow Christians in order to appease or ingratiate ourselves with unbelievers. We might call this the danger of winsomeness. Winsomeness, at its best, is seeking to remove unnecessary obstacles to the gospel. The classic text is 1 Corinthians 9, where Paul says that he has made himself a servant of all in order to win more of them. He becomes like a Jew to win Jews. He becomes like one outside the law to win those outside the law (though without stepping outside of the law of Christ). He becomes weak in order to win the weak. He becomes all things to all people in order to save some.

But this good desire to remove unnecessary obstacles can go wrong. Rather than trying to *win* our enemies, we often seek to *please* them, to pander to them, to coddle them. Rather than simply removing distractions from the gospel, we remove the offense of the gospel, paring down the rough edges so as not to alienate our audience. And we discover that one of the best ways to build bridges to unbelievers is to share their sympathies, their sensibilities, and their hostilities. Love what they love; hate what they hate. We find ways to communicate that "We're not like those Christians; we share your disgust at them." We forget that our deepest allegiance is to Christ and his people, even the members of his body that we regard as foolish and compromised.

To come at it another way, when winsomeness is elevated as *the* fundamental value, we become fixated on our reputation. In doing so, we cultivate cultural conditions conducive to manipulation. We hand our adversaries a steering wheel called "What We're Known For," and they hang our public image over our heads like the sword of Damocles.

I underscore the danger of being steered by our reputation because many Christians have misguided expectations on precisely this point. Many Christian leaders are prepared to be rejected by men and even persecuted for their faith in Christ, but they are not prepared to be rejected by men because of rank falsehoods, or because of guilt by association. But we must remember that there were people in the first century who really believed that Jesus was a drunkard and a glutton and demon-possessed, and that Paul was in it for the money and desired to tickle the ears of his hearers. In other words, Jesus and Paul were persecuted *by means of* rank falsehoods and lies. And we must be willing to cheerfully endure the same.

COWARDICE IS CONTAGIOUS

Finally, in Galatians 2 we learn that cowardice is contagious. Peter's fear leads him to withdraw, and the dominoes start to fall. His withdrawal spreads to the rest of the Jews, so that even Barnabas is led astray. Don't miss the significance of the word "even." This is Barnabas, son of encouragement, the one who risked his life and reputation to help draw the newly converted apostle Paul into the church in Acts 9. Peter's fear affects even him, so that he succumbs to the pressure and follows him into hypocrisy.

This simply reinforces the relationship between people-pleasing and man-fearing, between desiring the approval of men and fearing their disapproval. These are powerful passions, and they can overtake an entire community, especially when the leaders buckle. That's why, in Deuteronomy 20, in the midst of laws concerning warfare, God tells Israel, "And the officers shall speak further to the people, and say, 'Is there any man who is fearful and fainthearted? Let him go back to his house, lest he make the heart of his fellows melt like his own'" (Deut. 20:8). Fear does not just affect the one who is afraid. It spreads. It melts the hearts of others. It weakens and enfeebles a community so that it concedes what shouldn't be conceded and caves to worldly pressure.

LESSONS FROM PAUL

But not everyone caves. In the midst of this colossal failure of nerve, Paul stands out for his sober-minded courage and leadership. What can we learn from him?

First, note that Paul acts with purpose. He doesn't react; he responds. He's not another emotional domino that caves to pressure. Paul apparently has a high tolerance for the pain and discomfort of others.

This is an essential characteristic for leaders in the church. Leaders often intuitively know what actions will result in exasperated emails, frustrated phone calls, and painful conversations. It's tempting to avoid provoking such reactions and distress. But in order for growth and change to occur, leaders must be willing and able to press into conflict with a steady presence, and then maintain the stamina necessary to follow through in the face of resistance and sabotage.

Second, Paul takes a stand, and he does so publicly. Peter's error was public, and so Paul's correction is public. In taking this stand, Paul's primary goal is to bring clarity, to get beneath the fear and hypocrisy and pressure in order to reveal the fundamental issues for all to see. In other words, Paul is willing to talk about the elephant in the room. No obfuscation. No clouding the issue. Clear and direct speech that cuts to the heart of the matter. Peter's conduct is not in step with the truth of the gospel. This isn't simply about meal time; this is about whether Jesus has in fact torn down the dividing wall between Jew and Gentile. It's about whether the gospel message truly is Jesus + Nothing.

For leaders, this means that we should look for opportunities to move from submerged conflict to open conflict. Submerged conflict is frequently waged by subtle emotional and reputational pressure. Instead of seeking to persuade with arguments about what is true and good and wise, submerged conflict brings pressure to conform based on the feelings of an aggrieved group or the reputation of the community. Of course, in their place, emotions and reputation do matter. But they cannot substitute for rational and moral arguments. The shift to open conflict involves a candid and frank discussion of the underlying moral, theological, and prudential issues in play.

Third, Paul takes responsibility for himself, and expects others to do the same. He expects Peter to see his hypocrisy and own it. In confronting Peter publicly, Paul is risking escalation. But the risk is worth it. The conflict and confusion is already there. Nothing is gained by papering over it, by muttering "Peace, peace" when there is no peace.

The corollary of taking responsibility for one's actions is refusing to take the blame for the reactions of others. Because faithful leaders are willing to bring submerged conflict into the light, they are often accused of being the *cause* of that conflict. For example, the optical illusion at Antioch would be that Paul caused the conflict with Peter. But the truth is that Paul simply revealed the conflict and tensions that were already present, and thus he insists that Peter is the one who "stood condemned."

Fourth, Paul speaks differently to different groups, modeling both clarity and patience in this confrontation. He condemns committed heretics like the Troublers in Galatia, calling them false brethren and urging them to castrate themselves (Gal. 5:12). He rebukes hypocritical leaders like Peter, because like Moses to Aaron and Samuel to King Saul, Paul knows the importance of leadership. And he is patient with those who are confused and troubled by the whole mess, like the Christians in Galatia.

He also acts with prudence and wisdom throughout the situation. He resists the pressure to circumcise Titus (in Galatians 2:3) but is willing (in a different context) to circumcise Timothy in order to aid in gospel ministry. Paul is clear on first-order issues, recognizing how small compromises can threaten the foundation. But he also triages secondary issues, showing himself patient and long-suffering with various errors.

This patience and prudence flows from his maturity and sober-mindedness, from his heartfelt desire to please God. He is no pleaser of men, but a servant of Christ (Gal. 1:10). He was crucified with Christ, and therefore no longer lives, but Christ lives in him (Gal. 2:19–20). Keeping the approval of God ever before his face enables him to resist the attempts to steer and manipulate him by false accusations and guilt by association.

Though Paul doesn't record Peter's response to the confrontation in the book of Galatians, Acts 15 testifies to Peter's full acceptance of the Gentiles and his staunch resistance to the false brothers who would require them to be circumcised (Acts 15:5–11). By the grace of God, it seems that not only cowardice, but courage is contagious as well.

CHAPTER 6

COURAGE IN THE WORLD

IN THIS FINAL CHAPTER, WE MOVE OUT into the world. How should we conduct ourselves when we know we're going to face opposition and hostility from unbelievers? What do we do in the face of cultural chaos and social turmoil? To answer this question, we're going to explore Paul's final journey to Jerusalem in Acts 21–24.

Recall the situation as we pick up in Acts 21. Paul is on his way to Jerusalem, constrained by the Holy Spirit (Acts 20:22), trying to arrive by Pentecost (20:16). The Holy Spirit is testifying to him personally (20:23), and through other people (21:4, 10–12), that he is walking into imprisonment, affliction, and most likely death. Nevertheless, Paul is determined to go and finish his course there. So what do we learn from Paul's courageous example?

LESSON 1: AIM FOR PEACE

First, in facing opposition, Paul does not pick unnecessary fights. He labors to be at peace with all men, if at all possible. When Paul arrives in Jerusalem, the Christian leaders there rejoice in his news about the mission to the Gentiles. They then tell him that thousands of Jews in the area have come to faith in Christ, and that these new believers are being told by the enemies of the gospel that Paul is overthrowing Jewish customs (that he's saying, "Forsake Moses. Don't circumcise your kids. Don't walk according to the Jewish way of life"). And so they urge Paul to show these new Jewish converts that he has no problem with them continuing to live according to the customs of Moses, provided that they don't impose it on the Gentiles or view it as a requirement for salvation. And so Paul does. He goes to the temple; he pays for some other Jews to fulfill their purification offering. The goal here is to quell unnecessary hostility, to show that the Christians (and Paul in particular) are being misunderstood, misrepresented, and even slandered.

The lesson for us is simple: where we don't have to fight, we need not fight. Insofar as it depends on us, let us live at peace with all men. Christians must not be quarrelsome people. We must not give needless offense. When it comes to non-essential issues, we ought to be incredibly flexible. Paul believed that, in Christ, circumcision is nothing. Neither is uncircumcision. What counts is faith working through love. What counts is a new creation (Gal. 5:6; 6:15). So Paul's willingness to go to the temple and participate in this offering teaches us that we ought to try to live at peace with all men.

LESSON 2: KEEP YOUR HEAD WHEN CHAOS COMES ANYWAY

Second, when his peace-making efforts fail, Paul rolls with the punches. Paul's effort to clear things up for the Jews in Jerusalem doesn't work. Jews from Asia, where Paul had been ministering, see him in the temple and go ballistic (21:27). They repeat the slander ("This is the man who is teaching everyone everywhere against the people and the law and this place"), and jump to false conclusions, claiming that Paul brought a Gentile into the sacred place (21:28). In the end, they stir up a mob, seize Paul, and begin to beat him.

All Jerusalem is in confusion (21:30–31). The Roman tribune is notified, and when he arrives on the scene, he demonstrates that he is clearly in over his head. He comes upon a man being beaten by a mob and his solution is to arrest the victim (21:32–33). Crowds are shouting contradictory accusations; they are ready to get violent; chaos reigns. At that moment, Paul politely asks the tribune if he can have a word with him: "May I say something to you?" (21:37). At first, the tribune assumes that Paul must be some kind of revolutionary. He confuses Paul with an Egyptian insurrectionist. But Paul calmly tells him that he's a Jew from Tarsus, and requests permission to speak to the people.

Note this: there's a mob outside, ready to tear Paul to pieces. It's absolute chaos. The Roman soldiers appear unable to control the crowd. And Paul wants to give his testimony. "There's a violent mob outside? They want to kill me? Great. Can I have the mic?" The tribune sees a violent mob; Paul sees a potential congregation.

The amazing thing is that the tribune grants Paul's request. Paul's steadiness and sober-mindedness must have really shocked him, so much so that he grants Paul permission to speak.

So the second lesson for us is this. Even though we may not be looking for a fight, a fight may be looking for us, and we have to roll with the punches. Remember that the plan was to calm the tension in Jerusalem by accommodating the Jews, by becoming like one under the law in order to win those under the law. But five minutes in, and quelling hostility is out the window. Now we have a mob. But Paul just rolls with it. He is not thrown by the fact that his tactics failed. He keeps his head. He models sober-minded leadership in the midst of chaos. He sees an opportunity to preach the gospel, and he takes it.

LESSON 3: REBUKE APOSTLES OF THE WORLD WHILE PERSUADING REFUGEES FROM THE WORLD

Third, Paul speaks differently to different kinds of sinners. To understand what I mean, we must remember Paul's previous encounter with opposition in Acts 13. That chapter opens with the Holy Spirit commissioning Paul and Barnabas for their missionary work. They travel to Cyprus where they preach the word of God in the synagogues there. They arrive at Paphos, and the Roman proconsul (essentially a governor of a province) Sergius Paulus wants to hear what they have to say. So here's a prominent government official, a man of intelligence (13:7), who is eager to hear the word of God. But in his court there is a magician named Elymas, most likely a soothsayer who gets paid to predict the future. He opposes their preaching and tries to turn Sergius away from Christianity. Notice how Paul responds:

> But Saul, who was also called Paul, filled with the Holy Spirit, looked intently at him and said, "You son of the devil, you enemy of all righteousness, full of all deceit and villainy, will you not stop making crooked the straight paths of the Lord?" (Acts 13:9-10)

These are biting words, pointed words, sharp words directed at a particular person in public—and they originate from the Holy Spirit. In this case, the fruit of the Spirit is name-calling, insults, and harsh words.

This is not the only time we see this sort of Spirit-inspired insult. In Acts 7, Stephen is in almost exactly the same situation as Paul in Acts 21. He is accused of speaking "blasphemous words against Moses and God" (Acts 6:11). He is seized and hauled before the Jewish council, where false witnesses say, "This man never ceases to speak words against this holy place and the law, for we have heard him say that this Jesus of Nazareth will destroy this place and will change the customs that Moses delivered to us" (Acts 6:13-14).

In his defense, Stephen gives a redemptive-historical sermon, highlighting God's faithfulness to his promises despite Israel's idolatry. When he reaches the altar call, right at the climax of the sermon, he says, "You stiff-necked people, uncircumcised in heart and ears, resisting the Holy Spirit, persecuting the prophets; you temple-worshiping, idolatrous, Messiah-murdering lawbreakers" (Acts 7:51–53).

Given these two examples earlier in Acts, we might conclude that when we run into hostility to the gospel, we should unleash the spiritual insult. But then, when we come to Acts 21, we get surprised.

First, Paul shocks the crowd into silence by speaking flawless Hebrew (22:1–2)—they no doubt expected the Gentile-loving Greek-o-phile to speak only Greek. Second, he emphasizes their shared Jewish heritage: Paul was educated by Gamaliel (one of the most famous rabbis of his day) according to the strict traditions of their fathers (22:3a). Third, he emphasizes their shared zeal for God (22:3b). Notice this: he doesn't immediately identify their violence toward him with enmity toward the gospel; he gives them the benefit of the doubt and says, "I know that you're here today because you have a zeal for God. I completely understand, because I was educated according to that zeal for God and his law." Fourth, he emphasizes that he too once persecuted Christians, dragging them to prison and even supervising executions (22:4–5).

Shared language, shared heritage, shared zeal, shared persecution of Christians. Paul is effectively saying, "I get you. I was like you. I understand." He's building bridges. He's being winsome.

He then describes his encounter with the risen Jesus on the road to Damascus. This is the turning point of his life, and it's obvious what he is trying to do. "I was a persecutor like you, zealous for God. And then Jesus knocked me off my horse and redirected my zeal. I'm still zealous for God, but my zeal is shaped and formed by the death and resurrection of the Messiah for my sins." Even here he is trying to build bridges in order to persuade them. He emphasizes that Ananias, the Christian who came to restore his sight and baptize him, is "a devout man according to the law, well spoken of by all the Jews in Damascus" (22:12). In the midst of this, he weaves in the gospel: Jesus is the Righteous One (22:14). By calling on his name, Paul says, your sins can be washed away (22:16). He emphasizes that after his conversion, he came to the temple to pray. His Christianity didn't lead him to turn away from Jewish faith; it fulfilled his Jewish faith.

So how do we explain the difference between Paul's sharp words to the magician in Acts 13, and these winsome words to this mob in Acts 21? Why doesn't Paul preach like Stephen did when he was in a similar situation?

My argument is that Paul speaks differently to *apostles* of the world and *refugees* from the world. He rebukes the lying wolves, but patiently bears with the confused sheep. He condemns the misleaders but welcomes the misled.

A refugee is potentially persuadable. They might give the gospel a fair hearing if you can cut through the lies they've believed. Refugees come in all shapes and sizes. Some may be curious. Some may be seekers. Some may be wracked with guilt and shame (like the woman at the well in John 4). Some may be apathetic and uncaring. And some may be very hostile to the gospel because they've been lied to (like this mob). With such people, we ought to be long-suffering, patiently seeking to correct misunderstandings and clarify the truth.

Apostles of the world, on the other hand, have (at least) three defining characteristics. First, they are leaders in the world, whether official leaders like the priests and Sadducees, or unofficial leaders like the Pharisees and Elymas the magician. Wicked leaders such as these receive sharp and direct speech from Jesus and the apostles.

Thus, we ought to distinguish between angry and hostile people who have authority and influence, and angry and hostile people who don't. We shouldn't use satire and biting words on those who have little influence, or who have been deceived by those who know better. Remember King Lune of Archenland's maxim about mockery: "Never taunt a man save when he is stronger than you; then, as you please."[1] Don't punch down. But if you're Elijah surrounded by the king and his four hundred prophets of Baal, let it fly. If you're Stephen standing before the Sanhedrin who have heard the gospel multiple times from Peter and John, then pray for the words to speak, and testify clearly and courageously to the reality of their sin and the hope of Jesus.

Second, apostles of the world are on a mission. They prowl around looking for people to devour. Jesus accents this diabolical purpose in his indictment of the Pharisees: "Woe to you, scribes and Pharisees, hypocrites! For you travel

1. Lewis, *The Horse and His Boy*, 216.

across sea and land to make a single proselyte, and when he becomes a proselyte, you make him twice as much a child of hell as yourselves" (Matt. 23:14–15). Worldly apostles have a false gospel, and they are looking to spread it.

More than that, their mission includes preventing others from hearing and responding to the true gospel. Elymas is a clear example. The proconsul Sergius Paulus is eager to hear Paul's message. God has paved the way for Paul to give the gospel to Sergius. But Elymas is trying to make that straight path crooked. Or to change the metaphor, he's trying to build a wall between Sergius and the gospel. And Paul isn't having it.

So, when someone tries to build a wall between people and the gospel, sharp, pointed, exposing words are appropriate (and maybe even necessary) to tear it down. If Elymas didn't want to hear the gospel himself, that'd be one thing. But when he actively hinders others from hearing and responding, Paul tells the truth. He calls a spade a spade. "You there, building the wall, tearing up the path. You are a son of the devil. You are an enemy of all righteousness. You're a liar and a villain."

So also with Jesus and the Pharisees, Sadducees, and scribes. He does not treat them with kid gloves. He is not tender with them. He calls them names: a brood of vipers, sons of the devil, blind fools, and whitewashed tombs. In Matthew 23, he pronounces seven woes or curses on them because of their hostility to his ministry, and in those curses, he explains why his language is so sharp: "But woe to you, scribes and Pharisees, hypocrites! For you shut the kingdom of heaven in people's faces. For you neither enter yourselves nor allow those who would enter to go in" (Matt. 23:13).

Like Elymas, the Pharisees and scribes are preventing people from entering the kingdom. They keep the hungry from being fed by the word of God. And so Jesus doesn't play nice with them. Both Jesus and Paul love the sheep enough to protect them from wolves.

Third, apostles of the world are in the grip of high-handed rebellion. The Bible makes a distinction between stubborn defiance of God and what Leviticus calls "sins of error or thoughtlessness" ("unintentional sins" in the ESV). The distinction has to do with how we respond to our own sinfulness: do we dig in and persist, raising our fists to God in rebellion? Or are we grieved and broken by our sin (even if we haven't yet embraced Jesus to save us from it)?

So an apostle of the world is a leader on a mission, who is high-handed, defiant, and evangelistic in his rebellion, and who seeks to keep others from turning from their wickedness and entering the kingdom. When we encounter such people, then we can speak directly and sharply as the Spirit leads, especially if we are in a public setting like Paul in the court of Cyprus or Stephen before the Sanhedrin.

But that's not how Paul speaks to the mob in Acts 21. Their hostility doesn't awaken the Spirit's sharp words. So what does he do, surrounded as he is by an angry mob who has been stirred up by lies and slander, and who seems hell-bent on persecuting him? He tries to show them that even persecutors can be transformed. And they can do so without losing their zeal for the God of Israel. He's essentially saying, "I was like you. I thought zeal for God meant opposing and persecuting followers of Jesus. But then my story collided with Jesus, and he changed everything. Well, not everything. I'm still zealous for God. Christians are devout people with good reputations. But by calling on the name of Jesus, the Righteous One, my sins have been washed away. And yours can be too. You don't have to reject my testimony about Jesus."

LESSON 4: SHOW THEM HOW JESUS CHANGES EVERYTHING

And there's another lesson for us here: when we're confronted by a cultural conflagration, we need to help people see that they can be transformed by Jesus. When possible, we must identify with people and show them that at one time we were just like them. Liars, thieves, sexually immoral, homosexuals, drunkards, greedy: that's who we *were*. But we were washed, sanctified, and justified in the name of the Lord Jesus (1 Cor. 6:9–11). And our enemies can be too.

What's more, we need to help people to see what parts of their life must die for good, and what parts will be raised and transformed. As Bonhoeffer said, "When Christ calls a man, he bids him come and die." We must all die with Christ. But if we die with Christ, we will be raised, and some of our former life will be raised with us. Violence toward Christians must die for good. But the zeal for God beneath it—that can be transformed.

Our task is twofold: to help people to see where they are right now, and to help them see where they might be if Jesus collides with their story and transforms them like he's trans-formed us.

So Paul is speaking to this mob like refugees from the world, like those who have been misled by slander. He's becoming like a Jew in order to win them, identifying with them and their concerns and zeal in order to show them the way out of their sin. He's really trying to win them to Jesus.

But notice how Paul ends his sermon, and how the crowd reacts: "'And he [Jesus] said to me, "Go, for I will send you far away to the Gentiles."' Up to this word they listened to him. Then they raised their voices and said, 'Away with such a fellow from the earth! For he should not be allowed to live'" (Acts 22:21–22).

The crowd was listening to Paul; they were eating it up. Some of them may have begun to see themselves in Paul and been on their way to calling on Jesus. And then Paul has to go and spoil it by mentioning the inclusion of the Gentiles in the people of God. At this, the crowd again goes ballistic, and the sermon is over.

I'm confident that Paul knew good and well what reaction his words were likely to get. Remember what stirred this crowd up in the first place: they thought Paul brought a dirty Gentile into the temple (Acts 21:28–29). And yet, in his testimony, when he has the crowd hushed into silence listening to how Jesus changed his life, he says it anyway. He could've held off. He could have ended the sermon with, "I was like you. Now you can be like me. Call on Jesus. He'll wash away your sins and purify your zeal for

God." But he doesn't leave it there, because he *can't* leave it there. He has to be bold. He has to be clear and courageous about who Jesus is and what sin is.

LESSON 5: PREACH CLEARLY AND COURAGEOUSLY ABOUT SIN AND REPENTANCE

This is the fifth lesson for us, and it is a challenging one. It's easy to only preach the aspects of the gospel that people will like, to smooth over the rough edges so that we can win people to Jesus: "We'll talk about all of the hard truths after they believe. We'll call it 'discipleship'." But faithful leaders cannot do this. When we call people to repent of their sins, their bigotries, their idolatries, we cannot avoid the ones that we know will make them angry. God sent Jesus to bless us by turning every one of us from our wickedness (Acts 3:26). *Our* wickedness. The particular wickedness that belongs to us. You can't preach the gospel to a partying frat guy and not call him away from his drunkenness and debauchery. You can't preach the gospel to a practicing homosexual and not call him away from his sodomy. You can't preach the gospel to an antisemite without calling them away from their hatred of Jews. It may end the conversation. They may say, "Away with such a bigot." But faithfulness to Jesus means that we don't have the right to adjust the truth to suit their sin.

Think of it this way: our call is to testify to the truth, to witness to who Jesus is and what he has done. We hope and we pray that our witness and our testimony is persuasive, that God moves, and that people embrace the good news.

But our primary concern must be that our testimony and witness is faithful, regardless of whether it leads to conversion or rejection. We are the aroma of Christ among those who are being saved and those who are perishing, the aroma of life to life and the aroma of death to death (2 Cor. 2:15–17). So we cannot compromise, minimize, soften, or hide the truth in order to win converts. We must bear witness, regardless of the response.

LESSON 6: KNOW WHEN TO DE-ESCALATE AND WHEN TO PROVOKE

The conclusion of Paul's sermon highlights a sixth lesson: sober-minded leadership is adaptable to different circumstances. For instance, there are times when we aim to de-escalate a situation, to dial down the emotions in the pursuit of peace. This is especially true in personal relationships. When a family member erupts in anger, we remember that a soft word turns away wrath (Prov. 15:1). Love covers a multitude of sins (1 Pet. 4:8). As we saw in Chapter 4, sober-mindedness enables us to get curious about the other person's reactions. It helps us be patient and withdraw from the heated moment in order to pray and press in at a better time.

But in other situations, provocation is the order of the day. This is especially true in public and corporate settings when major issues are at stake. As we saw in the last chapter, Paul opposed Peter publicly at Antioch; he forced the issue into the foreground. And here in his sermon at Jerusalem,

Paul makes sure to include his calling to the Gentiles, knowing it will set off this particular crowd. In both cases, he provokes in order to bring clarity. He is willing to escalate matters and bring them to a head, rather than walk on eggshells and shrink back out of fear.

LESSON 7: STRATEGICALLY SEIZE PROVIDENTIAL OPPORTUNITIES

Paul's sober-mindedness enables him to see and take advantage of the providential opportunities that God sets before him. For example, when he is initially arrested, he obliquely tells the tribune that he is a "citizen of no obscure city" (that is, a citizen of Rome). The tribune, no doubt overwhelmed by the chaos of the moment, fails to follow up on the citizenship question (Acts 22:39). As a result, Paul is able to strategically make use of his Roman citizenship when the tribune later orders him to be flogged (22:24). Only after he has been stretched out to be whipped does he spring that particular piece of information on the tribune. The result is that the tribune is afraid because of his illegal detention and flogging (22:29), and, as we'll see, the Lord uses this fear to preserve Paul's life.

Paul's sober-mindedness enables him to exploit divisions among his opponents. At his trial before the Jewish council, he notices that both Pharisees and Sadducees are in attendance, and thus cries out, "I'm here because of the hope and the resurrection of the dead" (23:6), knowing that this will provoke a division among them. He rolls that little theological grenade in among his opponents and then ducks out of the way. The council, which had formerly been united against Paul, immediately falls into dissension, with the Pharisees now siding with Paul. The dissension grows violent, and the tribune, afraid that Paul (the Roman citizen) will be torn to pieces, rescues him (23:10).

After this the tribune takes great pains to protect Paul. He orders hundreds of soldiers to escort Paul to Caesarea to be questioned by Governor Felix after learning (again, providentially) that the Jews had bound themselves with an oath to deceive the tribune and ambush Paul on his way to the council (23:12–24). In other words, God uses Paul's shrewdness about his citizenship to preserve Paul's life. Of course, the tribune seeks to cover his mistakes, writing a letter to the Governor in which he says that he rescued Paul from the mob, "having learned that he was a Roman citizen" (23:27).

The lesson for us is this: if we're sober-minded, if we keep our heads and trust the Lord, we ought to expect surprising providences and strategically make use of them to advance the gospel. Like Paul, we can expect the Lord to stand by us (23:11), and therefore, we can take courage and testify at every opportunity.

LESSON 8: REJOICE IN THE FACE OF HOSTILITY AND PERSECUTION

Finally, Paul's sober-mindedness enables him to rejoice, even in persecution. When Paul is hauled before Governor Felix, he is falsely accused by the Jewish leaders (Acts 24:1–9). They claim that he is a plague, one who stirs up riots, and a profaner of the temple. In the face of such brazen false accusations, we might expect Paul to be angry. Instead, he says to Felix, "Knowing that for many years you have been a judge over this nation, I cheerfully make my defense." In other words, "I'd like to thank my accusers for this opportunity to give my testimony and preach the gospel yet again." No shrillness, no anger, no surprise, no bitterness—just cheerfulness in response to slander and persecution.

He maintains this cheerfulness even in the face of unjust imprisonment. Governor Felix, we discover, is a corrupt man. He keeps Paul in prison, despite lacking any legal reason to do so. He does give Paul some liberty while in custody; he makes sure his needs are cared for, and he regularly invites him to speak about Jesus. But none of this is noble. He wants Paul to offer him a bribe to get out of jail (24:26), and he keeps Paul in prison not because of justice, but because he's trying to do a favor for the Jewish leaders (24:27).

Despite the injustice, Paul is not embittered. He preaches the gospel to Felix often, focusing on righteousness, self-control, and the coming judgment, facts which apparently land with conviction on Felix who is alarmed by Paul's message (24:24–26; note that Paul continues to focus on the particular sins of his audience). Human injustice doesn't shake him. He believes in the coming judgment, and that God will put the world to rights.

So also with us. Persecution will come. Slanderers will bring their false accusations. At times they will be persistent, accusing us before every new audience. Like Paul, we must cheerfully defend ourselves when necessary, and make the most of the opportunities before us to commend Christ to everyone, from mobs, to tribunes, to governors, to Caesar.

STANDING ON THE ROCK

So we can conclude with this. Paul is returning to Jerusalem, knowing that affliction awaits him. He tries to live at peace with all men, but to no avail. Instead, he gets mobs and confusion, followed by illegal arrest, beatings, false accusations, and unjust imprisonment. But through it all, Paul is not shaken.

> When earth gives way and waters foam,
> When shadow falls on hearth and home,
> When nations rage and kingdoms mock,
> Then we stand on God the Rock.

Paul knows that he is standing on the Rock. He knows that God is writing his story. Not the Jewish leaders. Not the Roman tribune. Not the corrupt governor. And since Almighty God is writing his story, Paul is freed to look for every opportunity to say his lines, to witness, to testify to the grace of God in Christ.

May the same be true for us. God is writing our story. Not the Supreme Court. Not Congress. Not the President. Not Big Business, Big Education, or Big Tech. God is. Jesus is. Which means our call is to be wise as serpents: to think strategically, to plan well, to make use of every righteous means available to advance the gospel. Our call is to be innocent as doves: to live at peace with all men if possible, but without compromising the truth, or shrinking back out of fear. Our call is to be cool as a cucumber: to remain unshaken by our adversaries, ready to roll with it when our plans come unraveled, confident, humble, and secure in the midst of mayhem, because we know that Christ is risen, reigning, and working for our good.

CONCLUSION

YOUR HOME, YOUR CHURCH, AND THIS world need leaders who are mature and sober-minded, filled with gravity and gladness, and grounded in the glory of Jesus. Becoming that sort of leader is a lifelong work of God's grace in us and through us. In light of that, it seems good to close this little book with some exhortations to help you cultivate the kind of steadiness and sober-mindedness that honors Christ and blesses your people.

First, get clarity on what God wants from you and the institutions you lead. This includes your calling as a human, as a Christian, as a husband and father, in your church, in your vocation, and in the world. This clarity comes from knowing what the mission is and isn't. Labor to keep your various missions before your mind, lest you be distracted and derailed by trials and challenges.

Second, learn to recognize your own angst. Pray for God to search your heart, and be alert to your frustrations, hesitations, reluctances, anxieties (Ps. 139:23–24). Cultivate the kind of self-awareness that knows when you are tensing up or shutting down, getting intense or checking out.

Third, grow in your awareness of the anxiety, tension, and angst in your home, at your job, and in your church. Identify the crackle in the room. Learn to detect the ways that the passions out there stoke the passions in your own heart. In particular, be alert to the presence or absence of playfulness in your family, your workplace, and your church. Playfulness is a sign of high trust, humility, and health, and its absence is almost always a sign that reactive passions have hardened into an ungodly intensity.

Fourth, as you grow in this awareness, seek God's help in getting a grip on yourself first. Take responsibility for your own actions and reactions. Steady yourself by directing your mind to God's fatherly care for you, the glory of your calling as a Christian, and the particular duties that God has laid upon you. Refuse to simply be another emotional domino that amplifies the reactive anxieties in your community. Instead, let your reasonableness be known to all.

Fifth, aim for clarity in whatever room you find yourself in. Keep your head. Cut through the fog. Often this will mean de-escalating tensions in private. But when passions are spilling over in the public, you may be called upon to cheerfully provoke a reaction in order to bring necessary clarity for others. So pray for wisdom and then aim for clarity.

Sixth, act with steady and patient purpose. Lean into conflict with stability of soul. Have nerve. Take heart. Be strong and courageous. Refuse to succumb to emotional manipulation, and help others to see where they are walking on eggshells in order to avoid confrontation.

Seventh, grow in the stamina necessary to endure blowback. Keep your head when everyone else is losing theirs and blaming it on you. When you detect sabotage and manipulation, be absolutely unsteerable, but instead patiently and intentionally press forward. Refuse to see responsibility as a zero-sum game. Maturity means taking responsibility for your actions, attitudes, and emotions. Lead the way, and call others to follow.

Eighth, calibrate yourself by other faithful Christians. Be humble and willing to receive correction. When you receive a rebuke or a challenge driven by what is true and good and wise according to the Scriptures, be the most reasonable person in the room, ready to admit mistakes and change course in response to new information.

Ninth, remember that the grace of God defines you. The grace of God makes you who and what you are. As the apostle Paul says, "by the grace of God I am what I am" (1 Cor. 15:10). God's grace is not in vain but works in us so that we possess a steady, joyful presence as we guide others with gravity and gladness.

Finally, brothers, be steadfast, immovable, always abounding in the work of the Lord, knowing that in the Lord your labor is not in vain (1 Cor. 15:58).